CLASSROOM MANAGEMENT 101

A Step-By-Step Guide to Quiet a Noisy
Class, Quell Bad Behavior and Restore a
Positive Environment Through Practical
Tips and Easy-to-Follow Strategies

By Oliver Hanson

TABLE OF CONTENTS

INTRODUCTION

It's Monday morning and you're off to class. As soon as your students start filing into the room, they're laughing and bouncy, hyped from their weekend fun. You call for them to quiet down and most of them do, but then they erupt in giggles when one student cracks a joke. It's a common problem for teachers and if you don't have your classroom under control, it can drastically affect what your students learn.

As a teacher, you have the opportunity to change lives. However, a room full of unruly students can also change you and may even make you regret becoming a teacher. When everything is out of control and you aren't sure how to correct it, you'll find it very difficult to enjoy your job, much less do it well.

Your students are children, whether you teach elementary, middle school, or high school. Children will always test the limits, since that's what they do. It's part of their way of learning how to do things and seeing just what is acceptable. This is something that you're not going to change . . . but how you handle it is most definitely under your control.

Well-behaved students aren't just easier to teach, they actually learn better. There are fewer distractions and you've taught them to focus on the lesson, rather than their friends. This is an important part of teaching, since the lessons you impart in your classroom will stay with them for years to come.

And yet, it seems impossible to have a well-behaved group of children! This is particularly true after an exciting event or holiday, or when you have a large number of students. More and more classrooms are becoming overcrowded, thanks to a variety of factors. This makes it even more challenging to manage your students.

From Jungle to Learning Environment

Over the years, I've heard quite a few people refer to their classroom as a zoo or a jungle. The purpose of this book is to take your classroom from jungle to the ideal learning environment. You will learn to be a better teacher, someone who is able to immediately bring their class to order and maintain that order.

If you're thinking that this is impossible, since your students already learned all the bad habits, don't stress. I'll be showing you exactly how to reverse those bad habits and get your students back in line so they can enjoy being in your classroom and learn more. Those eager little brains are looking for knowledge and stimulation, but they aren't yet disciplined enough to make it happen. You're the one who needs to take charge.

Imagine walking into your classroom and seeing the children file in quietly, finding their seats, taking out their books and papers without throwing spitballs or crumpled notes. Imagine a class that listens attentively while you speak, raises their hands to respond in an orderly fashion, and lines up neatly to leave the classroom, without shoving each other or leaving their desks in disarray. It sounds too good to be true, right?

Fortunately for you, this is not too good to be true. I've seen classroom after classroom transformed by the tips I'm going to give you in this book.

Whether you are a brand new teacher or a jaded one who has years under their belt, you'll find something of use in these pages.

Who Am I?

You might be wondering who I am to be writing this book and speaking with such authority, so let me introduce myself. I'm Oliver Hanson. I'm a math teacher and over the years, I've taught hundreds of students. Needless to say, I wasn't the popular teacher, since math is a much-detested subject. Students hated me simply based on the nature of my lessons, so I needed a solution. Something to make math more palatable and myself a little more exciting, too.

I am passionate about teaching and have been since I was a child. There was never any doubt that I would go into teaching. My mother was a teacher and from an early age, I got the chance to see how she changed lives. It made me want to do that, too, but I never anticipated the hate that a math teacher would receive!

To say that my first year as a teacher was a disaster would be a bit of an understatement. While I love teaching and brought my passion for both my students and my subject to the classroom, it wasn't enough. That's something I learned early on. No matter how dedicated you are, if you can't get your students to settle down and engage, you have no business teaching them. That may sound harsh, but I also believe that every teacher can learn to manage their classroom.

I wrote this book because I want to show other teachers that, with a little training, you can love this job as much as you did before you set foot in a classroom. It is, without a doubt, the most beautiful, satisfying job in the world and I would never choose anything else.

You Can Become a Better Teacher

When you have a well-behaved class, it's a joy to walk into your classroom every day. You won't feel defeated or stressed, you'll be excited about going to school. The sense of satisfaction at the end of a great day with your students can't be underestimated . . . it's something you won't get in any other job.

I strongly feel that there are three core characteristics for building a relationship with your students. These are trust, respect, and admiration. In this book, you'll train yourself with the top techniques and learn the best strategies for classroom management. Put them into action and your class will be loyal and dedicated for as long as you teach them.

I've had teachers thank me for teaching them the techniques I'm about to reveal to you. This is information that has changed teaching lives, as well as students. Teachers who come to me, tired, burned out, and ready to quit because teaching is just too hard have told me that with my advice, they're able to build deeper, more meaningful relationships with their students and manage their classroom. Teaching has become a joy for them once more.

Don't worry, I may be a math teacher, but I'm not teaching rocket science here. The techniques and strategies that I'll show you how to implement are easy enough that anyone can apply them and get results. It's surprisingly easy to turn it all around.

What to Expect from This Book

By the time you finish this book, you will be completely equipped with the knowledge and skills you need to turn your classroom into a respectful, easy to manage space. However, it doesn't happen automatically.

While I am giving you everything you need to change the way you teach, YOU are the one who has to take action. You've probably heard the saying "old habits die hard." It's dramatically true and the sooner you start changing habits, both yours and your students', the sooner you'll see changes.

Read this book and immediately start implementing the information given here. It's very important that you begin to take action now.

Everything you need to know about classroom management is at your fingertips. Read, learn, and apply. You'll be amazed at the results.

CHAPTER 1

THE KEY TO EFFECTIVE CLASSROOM MANAGEMENT

I'd been teaching for a few years when Jack (not his real name) came into my class. He was 12 years old, with all the attitude that comes with the changing hormones and sudden growth spurts at that age. He was, in short, a teacher's worst nightmare.

Jack disrupted every class he was in. He hated math and made sure everyone knew it. He talked loudly, interrupted my lessons to make jokes about the material and turned every single one of my math classes with him into a long session of trying to get him to quiet down so I could teach. I resorted to punishments, sending him to the principal's office, assigning extra homework (which was never done), and giving him detention. Nothing worked. He was as unruly and belligerent as ever.

One day, I noticed that Jack tended to come into school earlier than the rest of the kids. He usually hung out in the hallway, chewing gum, horsing around, and being a pest. When he saw me looking at him out there in the hall, he moved his act into my classroom.

It took a week of sending him out of my room early in the morning to curb his active behavior. Then something happened. Just as I was at my lowest point as a teacher, realizing that this one kid had defeated everything I had learned about keeping my students under control and making me feel like a failure, Jack stopped doing flips over desks and came and sat on the edge of my desk. I was about to kick him out when he asked me why I'd become a teacher.

That's the big question, isn't it? But it's pretty rare to hear a kid ask something like that. I explained how my mother had been a teacher and how I really wanted to make a difference. Then he asked me why I taught math, of all things.

Every morning, Jack would come and perch on my desk and ask questions. He wanted to know everything about me, from my family life to my professional life. He wanted to know if I enjoyed teaching (that was doubtful at that point) and if I would choose something else if I could start over. Then he started to talk about himself.

I learned that Jack, rowdy, trouble-causing, joke-cracking Jack, was an orphan. He lived with his aunt and her boyfriend. His torn jeans weren't the result of some weird fashion trend, but due to the lack of money in his family. He came into school early because he hated to be at home with his aunt's boyfriend.

Bit by bit, the reality of Jack's life came out and as he started to trust me more, he also started to focus in class. To my surprise, he all but stopped with the jokes and started raising his hand to ask questions to clarify what I was teaching. Something had drastically shifted in our relationship and once

I realized what had happened, I was able to apply it to my other students, as well.

Building Relationships to Build Your Classroom

See, your students crave a connection. When they first walk into that classroom, you're just a random person, there to tell them what to do. If you build a relationship with them, though, they will see that you respect and care about them and they will, in turn, respect and care about you. Not all kids are easy. Jack took weeks before he started to open up to me . . . but I also didn't realize how important that connection was for him.

Earlier, I mentioned that one of the core principles of effective classroom management is building relationships. This is exactly where you need to start. Creating a rapport with your students will enable you to teach more effectively and you'll find that they also pay better attention in class and respond better to your corrections.

It's been shown that when a teacher cultivates a relationship with their students, the students have a better sense of belonging. It can actually reduce bullying and help students feel more at home.

We've all seen those feel-good movies where teachers turn an entire class around simply by caring. While it's not quite as easy as it might seem on screen, those movies are based on real-life actions of amazing teachers who made it their mission to connect with even the most challenging students. It is possible and it does change lives. In fact, it will change you as much as it changes your students, so be ready for your life to be different, too.

Steps to Building a Relationship with Your Students

Your students are all individuals and that means one approach won't work for everyone. However, I have found that being positive and upbeat tends to break down even the most stubborn student. Of course, it's tough to actually act that way when you're annoyed and frustrated with a student's behavior, but persistence is key.

Here are the steps to building a relationship with your students:

Step One: Get Personal

Share information about yourself and your personal life. Don't just share your strengths, but also let some of your weaknesses show. I know this is one of those sketchy areas where most teachers say that showing weakness is like chumming the water where sharks lurk, but I've found it to be effective. In fact, it is far more effective than if you pretend only to be strong and never let your students see that you are, indeed, human.

No one can relate to someone who is always perfect. It's our flaws that make us relatable and this is particularly true when it comes to difficult students. After all, they are used to adults in their lives letting them down, so it is best that you show them you know you have flaws. Teach them that it's okay to be vulnerable.

Making yourself somewhat vulnerable allows your students to identify with you. They are at a stage in their life where things can be tough and you don't always know about their history or home life. However, when they hear that you also face trouble, they can identify with that and will be more likely to connect with you.

Step Two: Spend Time Getting to Know Them

It may seem silly to get to know students that you may never see again, but you have one school year to make a difference and the best way to do that is to really connect. You can only do this if you have a chance to interact individually with them.

I like to schedule one-on-one meetings, while observing the necessary school guidelines, of course, with my students. These are simple times where they can share what they're struggling with and we can talk about both schoolwork and home life or what is going on in their personal life. These meetings generally start off a bit awkwardly, because the student is not sure they can trust me yet. However, as time goes on, they learn that they can trust me.

Once a student starts to trust, they start to open up and share their life. That's when you have made a connection and can build on it. With Jack, I accidentally built this connection, but now I do it deliberately with each of my students.

Step Three: Give the Reins to the Students

I love to have my students lead activities or self-direct activities from time to time. Not only does it give me a chance to see how well they understand the material, but it also lets them know that I trust them. This can help build some loyalty, but it's also an excellent way to empower your students. They feel more secure that they can handle the material when you let them take over.

This tends to be something I do a little later in the year, once the relationships have already bloomed a bit and they've had time to learn some of the class material. Then we start doing projects where they need to put their knowledge to use.

Following these steps will help you create amazing connections with your students and they will be far more likely to pay attention in class. When you speak to them, they'll pay attention, because they know you value and respect them.

Step Four: Look for Opportunities to Connect

Students may not view you as someone they can get to know, particularly in the beginning. If they've had poor experiences previously with their teachers, they aren't going to be very forthcoming early on. It's up to you to make sure that the opportunity to connect is there and to take advantage of it.

This can take most of the first semester. Be patient, because there are always opportunities to create a bond with each student, but it can take time. Often, you need to try and try again multiple times before the student will actually respond in a positive way. Once you've got their attention, though, you can really start to work with them.

There are opportunities to connect throughout the day. You can find them when the students enter the room, leave the class, or when they arrive early. Even running into a student in the hallway and asking how they're doing will close the normal teacher-student distance and help them see you as a human being who needs to connect.

Tips for Building Relationships

Still not entirely sure how to get started with making a connection? Why not start with a smile and a greeting. We've all seen those viral videos with teachers greeting children at the classroom door and allowing them to choose what sort of greeting they want. This works with older kids, too, who may not be interested in choosing a hug or high five. Just being there to smile and greet them is enough to give them the feeling that you appreciate them coming.

Other ideas include:

Host classroom events. These don't need to be related to your subject, though they certainly can be. A classroom event should be a fun experience, something out of the norm that will wake everyone up. You can do these on a regular basis, such as the last school day of each month, every third Friday, etc. The idea here is to set up an expectation and a situation where your students can be themselves. The shakeup from the normal classroom atmosphere will also revitalize them.

Recognize them. Kids are like anyone else, they love to be recognized for their achievements. Just make a point of letting them know that you noticed their hard work. It doesn't need to be specifically learning-related, though. If you see a student modeling kind behavior, such as lending a pencil to another student or offering to help clean up after class, thank them for being kind. You should always praise behavior you want to see more of, regardless of whether or not it is directly related to your class.

Give them notes. Students are used to getting notes that reprimand them, or notes to take home to their parents, where they get into trouble for something they've done at school. I've seen so many parents who already think the worst of their unruly children. They automatically assume that any teacher is going to have something unpleasant to say about their child. When you praise them, it not only changes the student's view of themselves, but their parents' view of the child. I love to give kids encouraging notes saying how impressed I am that they took the time on a project, or that I know this is difficult, but I'm proud of how hard they are working. These notes should focus on the attention and work the student is putting in, not their brains. This encourages them to work harder and makes them realize that they can do it.

Involve their parents. Connecting with a student's parents can help you connect with the student. This means building up the student in front of the parents, however, to help them feel stronger and abler. The parents will be proud of their child and this can have a positive impact on the child in more ways than one. You can actually help a student bond better with their parents in this way, too.

Take the time to really get to know your students deeply, and you'll see drastic improvements in the way they act in class. It's far easier to manage a classroom full of students who like and respect you than a group of rowdy kids who couldn't care less what you think of them.

CHAPTER 2

HOW YOU START THE YEAR IS HOW THE YEAR WILL CONCLUDE

Chances are you've been taught to use methods of teaching that focus on getting kids to learn from the curriculum. However, the idea of a growth mindset is something that we're seeing more and more of in the world of education. It's not uncommon to find teachers set on developing a growth mindset in their students, but they still remain on a fixed mindset themselves. How can you change this to make it work for you?

First, you need to look at what it means to have a growth mindset.

Most people feel they must get things done correctly the first time, but when you have a growth mindset, you are focused on the process of learning, rather than the end result. This makes it okay to make a mistake. Instead of considering it a failure, you can consider it part of learning and try again. The growth mindset is one where intelligence, abilities, and personal qualities can be developed and improved. The fixed mindset says that these are already determined and cannot be changed.

A positive method of thinking is essential for both teachers and students and should be used to encourage learning and picking yourself back up after a failure. This is an essential skill that will serve your students (and you) well in the future. We can all benefit from learning from our failures.

Growth Mindset for Teachers

How can you, as a teacher, cultivate a growth mindset for yourself. We'll look at how you can do this for the students in a minute, but first, you need to look at yourself. You will be modeling the behavior for your students, so it's important that you make sure you are focused on this yourself.

Listen to Everyone

Every single person you meet, old or young, has a story to tell. They have something you can learn from and all you need to do is be willing to listen. Listening is a skill that we could all stand to develop a little more. You expect your students to pay attention and listen, so make sure you are doing the same.

Think back to the last time you were in a meeting. Did you listen carefully to the speakers or were you thinking about what you needed to do when you got home, counting the minutes until the meeting let out, or thinking about lunch? It's normal for our minds to wander, but you need to learn to actually listen if you want to pick up more information over time.

You might need to figure out some ways to help you stay focused when you're listening to something that doesn't necessarily interest you. Taking notes is one way to do this. You can implement other methods to help you learn more from other people, as well.

Experiment with New Ideas

It's one thing to learn new things and listen to others, but are you actually implementing any of it? Part of being a great teacher is experimenting with new ideas. There's nothing wrong with letting your students know that it's an experiment, either. They will be interested to see how it turns out, just like you are.

Without innovation, we cannot grow and improve our world. Your classroom is your world and it's the perfect place to start opening up and finding new ideas that you can implement. You'll find that no single method of teaching is perfect. That's why you should always be trying new things and seeing how they work. Use bits and pieces from various methods of teaching and you might be surprised at how well they work in your classroom. After all, if you don't try, you can't learn whether something will work.

Keep Learning

A fixed mindset will be stuck on just repeating what has worked for the most part in the past. If you want to grow, you need to learn. Learning should be something that you always do. We are naturally curious creatures, so use that curiosity to expand your knowledge and find new ways to do things. Part of that is reading this book. You obviously picked it up because you wanted to make sure you were doing the best by your students. You wanted to learn classroom management techniques and now you are.

Reading books like this one is a great way to learn. You can also join forums or groups where teachers share ideas, read blogs and articles to learn new techniques, and talk with other teachers about their ideas. It doesn't have to end with what you learned in school. You can also model this for your students. Tell them what you've been learning or tell them that you'll look something up after they've told you a new fact. Let them know that even adults are still learning and normalize it for them. The more you show them how to learn, the more interested they will be in learning on their own.

Ask More Questions

This is a great way to teach your students that it's okay to be curious and want to learn. It's also an excellent way to actually learn more on your own. Most of us start out in life with a lot of curiosity. Just listen to a preschooler constantly asking "Why?" They don't let a train of thought float by without grabbing on and riding it to the very end. We lose that as we get older and that's a shame.

It's time to bring back the habit of asking questions. You can use it with your students. When they answer something, ask them why. Get them to explain their thought process. You'll get them to think more about it and you'll find yourself thinking more, too.

Questions aren't just for the classroom, though. You can use them anywhere. Ask more questions in life for the next week and see how much more you grow as a person. Then turn around and apply that to your students.

Stay Flexible

If you want to see growth, both in yourself and in your classroom, you need to be flexible. Not all students are the same and you may find that you need to make some adjustments to include everyone.

Don't get stuck in one way of thinking. That's the best way to become obsolete. You probably have had at least one teacher in your life who was unable to keep up with the times and stayed fixed on a certain mindset. That is the teacher you don't want to be. Stay open to the possibilities of new things and make sure you are open to innovative ideas. You can learn a lot from your students if you stay flexible.

Pick Up New Tech

The world is changing rapidly and you probably have noticed that new technology is pouring out faster than you can adapt. It's important that you do adapt, however. The latest technology, social media trends, and apps are what your students are into and it is to your benefit to learn these things, too.

When you know what kids are talking about, you can join in the conversations. You'll be able to work your curriculum around the current interests and enjoy a better rapport with your students.

Your growth as a teacher will have a significant impact on your students. Stay open to opportunities as they present themselves and take advantage of your ability to grow and learn.

Start the Year Off On the Right Foot

When you begin a new school year, you probably start off with expectations for the students. You may even have a reward system for the best students and the hardest workers.

Some common reward systems include:

- Assigning kids a clip that moves from the red zone to the green zone and students in the green zone receive prizes at the end of the week.
- Rewarding the top grade with a special prize.
- Giving the best performer in class their choice of seats.
- Having a list of the "bad" kids on public display.
- Giving top students a "student of the week" space.

While these reward systems can be quite effective for your best students, they tend to discourage the ones who have a harder time in school. They will tend to find it more discouraging than anything, particularly after they have seen the same students getting the prizes time after time. If you want to truly encourage all your students, you need to find a different way to give them a boost.

Remember that you want to encourage a growth mindset in your students, not a fixed one. You want them to realize that with hard work, anyone can reach their goals. Some people may need to work harder in certain areas, but everyone has their strengths.

Your students will need to learn some specific lessons when it comes to the growth mindset. Depending on their age and how many people before you have taught them that results are all that matters, you may have your work cut out for you. That's just fine, though. You will see a dramatic improvement in their behavior when you teach the following core concepts:

We learn from our mistakes: This is something that every student must know. Use famous examples, like Thomas Edison failing over 2,000 times before he invented the light bulb. Students need to understand that they should expect to make mistakes and fail sometimes, but that it isn't the end of the world. You can model this, even making mistakes on purpose to show them that it just isn't that big of a deal. Sit down and discuss how you can do things differently now that you know what you know.

We help each other: Your classroom should be a space where students learn to help one another. If someone is struggling, in their life or in their classwork, you can help the kids brainstorm how they can help that person. When they start to work as a class to aid each other, they are building crucial skills for the future.

We are trustworthy: Show your students that you trust them. Let them know that they are responsible for the outcome of the class. You can help them out by presenting choices and having them select the one. Let them know that you trust them to make the best decision. An example of this would be if a student is failing. You could offer them the opportunity to make up their grades and ask them to choose a project they think would be worth the extra points. If need be, offer two options and let them select between these, though many students can come up with their own project. They will own their choice and will be more likely to complete the project on time and correctly.

We understand the results of our behavior: This is an area that most teachers will need to spend some extra time teaching. Students need to understand that what they do has a consequence, good or bad. You can brainstorm some good and bad consequences for different types of behavior, like bullying, tutoring someone else, etc. These scenarios are great for getting students to think outside of themselves, too.

We believe in growth: Teach your students to celebrate each other's hard work. When you see a student self-correct, let them know that you noticed they stopped their behavior and changed it. Congratulate them on improving themselves and make it a celebration. It's a good way to let students know that making a mistake isn't fatal, but that learning from it is important. You can even ask students to self-evaluate at the end of each month and to come up with ways they've improved over time.

Take the time to work with your students in changing their attitudes and outlook. If you are the first teacher to do this with them, you'll probably be met with some resistance, particularly from older students. However, it is well worth the time you take to help your class change to a growth mindset. Here are a few other ways to get the ball rolling:

Eliminate Negative Self Talk

I'm sure every teacher has heard a student wail something negative about themselves at some point, though this may be more common in math class. Things like:

- "I can't do it."
- "It's too hard for me."
- "I'm too stupid to do this."
- "I'm dumb."

Our job as teachers is to turn that negative self-talk into something positive. Mindset really does make a difference and when your student is convinced that they are too stupid to learn, they're just not going to learn.

How can you turn this around? There are a few ways, but first, you need to realize that the child has probably heard these things being said to them before. Their inner voice is inherently negative and that can be a complicated thing to change. It is possible, but you need to replace the negative talk with something else.

Encourage students to pick a mantra that they can repeat. You can offer several options for them to choose from. These may include:

- "I've got this."
- "I get better every day."
- "Every problem has a solution."
- "Mistakes are learning opportunities."
- "I believe in myself."
- "I can do this."
- "I can do anything."

Students can also choose their own mantra, of course, as long as it is positive and uplifting. Next, encourage them to repeat it to themselves whenever bad thoughts pop into their heads. You won't always hear the student say they're too dumb for something, but they are thinking it. Remind them to think of their mantra and to repeat it when they are struggling. This can really help your students redirect their thoughts and focus on solving the problem.

Tell Them to Ask for Help

In a classroom, your students have no good reason to get frustrated and stuck. After all, they have a teacher right there. We're taught that asking for help is a weakness, but this is something that needs to be eliminated, particularly in your classroom.

Encourage your students to come to you if they don't understand something. That's what you're there for and you can often correct their confusion with a simple explanation. Students should always feel free to ask for aid when they need it. This can also help you build a relationship with your students, since they know they can rely on you to explain things to them.

Encourage Hard Work

You want your students to work hard at what they're doing. This is where you should be encouraging them, not when they hit a high mark or reach a specific goal. It's tough to struggle when other people around you understand things faster and better than you do. Kids who learn early on that they need to work hard to reach their goals will be far more successful in life, though, so you want to teach them to do just that.

Instead of being the slave driver, always pushing students to work more, you can let them do this for themselves. Many students will respond positively to being responsible for their own success, though this is an area that you will have to work on overtime.

A simple way to encourage them to work well and check their own progress is to create a wall poster that shows the steps they need to follow on each paper. For example, I have one that says:

Did you . . .

1. Show your work?
2. Explain your answer?
3. Follow the proper protocol?
4. Sign your work?
5. Finish every question?

Students can easily look at the poster and check their own work. If they turn something in that is not finished, I'll ask them if they have gone through the steps and request they look again. This puts the correction on the student and I don't have to constantly remind them to put their name on their work or show their work.

Build Teamwork

Students all have different abilities and the traditional reward systems can end up creating a divide between the top students and the ones who need to work harder. I like to bridge that divide by creating teams and putting students together with other students who have the opposite abilities.

For example, I'll team up four kids who have differing abilities in math. One may be very logical, while another is a creative thinker. One might have persistence and patience, while another is eager to find the solution immediately. You really have to know your students in order to make this work, but it can end up being the best thing you've done for your class.

Once the students are put into teams, they are required to work together on a project. Ideally, the project will require all their abilities and talents and they'll need to utilize their strengths in order to get the end result. This helps the students realize that everyone is useful and that they all have their own abilities. It also allows students to coach each other in their area of expertise. For example, if one student is very good at algebra, they might help another student understand. I always emphasize working together, rather than one person running out in front.

A fun way to incorporate this into your classroom is through escape room scenarios. You can team up as many as eight students at a time and they have to follow the clues to "escape." Kids love this scenario and you can create clues that use things you've been learning in class. The students will need to work together to solve the clues and escape before class is over.

Focus on Self-Improvement

Have your students evaluate themselves after the first month or so of school. This gives them some time to learn your methods and to start to understand the whole idea of growth through mistakes.

They don't need to share this information with the rest of the class if they don't want to, but they should mark on a scale of 1-10 how well they're doing in specific areas of their life. You can focus entirely on school if you like, but I've found it most effective to have students evaluate their lives in general. It takes the exercise out of the classroom and helps them understand how applying the growth mindset to the rest of their lives can work, as well.

Areas that I like to focus on include:

- Relationships
- Classroom Behavior
- Overall Behavior
- Classwork
- Homework
- Attitude
- Social Life

Of course, you can add anything you feel is relevant here. Most students will be happy to work on this project and especially if they don't have to share it with anyone. They can also mark where they would like to be with each area of their lives.

With a growth mindset, you can ensure that both you and your students are learning as much as possible. Instead of instilling a fear of failure, you can build up their interests and help them become more responsible. Trust and confidence in your students will only help them feel better about themselves. They will start to strive to reach your expectations of them, because you are empowering them to do just that.

CHAPTER 3

CLASSROOM MANAGEMENT FOUNDATIONS

Teaching requires many skills beyond simply standing in front of the class and talking. While it's easy enough to do that, teaching itself is not necessarily easy.

Skills for Modern Teachers

Nowadays, teachers are called upon to do far more than ever before. If you have been teaching for more than a few days, you have already discovered that you need to take an active part in helping students learn. It's not always simple, but you'll need some special skills to keep on top of things in the classroom.

Some of the skills you'll need to develop as a teacher include:

Spread Positivity

It's essential that you be a positive light in the classroom and in your students' lives. School is hard enough and if you can be positive for them, it will spread. Soon you'll find that students smile when they come into your classroom, because they know that this is a positive space.

How can you spread positivity? Try one of these methods:

Smile frequently. A smile is the best way to make those around you feel happy and comfortable, so use it. The power of smiling is highly underrated and you'll notice that most students will smile back at you.

Praise them. Let students know that you appreciate them. Give them individual compliments like, "Good job, Damian, you worked hard on this and it shows." or "You've improved your attitude so much, Jessica! It's wonderful to see." Kids like to hear great things about themselves and if you praise the hard work they've done, you'll promote a growth mindset, too.

Keep a journal. This is for yourself, but it will help you be happier in class. Take the time to write down something about that troublesome child in your class that is pleasant. What is good about them? This exercise can help you focus on the good things and see the student in a different light.

Write notes. Write a note to one child each day and give it to them. These notes should be filled with positive things. It can be as simple as "Your smile lights up the room!" to "I am so proud of you for helping Henry today." This lets the kids know that you are paying attention and notice the things they do. It can be just the boost your students need.

Share the positive. When a student does something great, or helpful, be sure to spread that story around. Tell other teachers, share on a blog or social media, and basically just make it something that other people can feel good about, too.

Create a "say something nice" board. In your classroom, set up a bulletin board with a stack of colored notes and a few pens. Encourage students to write something nice about someone else and post it on the board. This could be something they noticed another student doing that was neat, or it could just be "Anna has a great personality!" Students will find themselves checking the board and feeling special when they read something about themselves. Make sure to include the less-mentioned students yourself, if need be.

You rock circle. Is a student having a rough time? Are they acting out unusually? Why not have a "you rock" circle? Sit the student in the middle of the circle of kids and have everyone take a turn saying something positive about the student. I actually enjoy doing these randomly, just picking a student and having a rock circle for them. It's a terrific confidence booster.

You are responsible for the overall atmosphere in your classroom, so make it count. Spread that positivity.

Attitude is Everything

When you walk into the school in the morning, what is your attitude like? Are you grumpy? Dreading another day cooped up in a classroom? Or are you happy and excited for the new day? Eager to see your students again and share information with them?

Your attitude will make or break your class. It doesn't just affect you, it affects everyone in the room. If you come in with a bad attitude, your students will pick up on that and will quickly start acting out. Kids can sense your attitude from a mile away.

You want to be positive and make sure you can spread that positivity, as mentioned previously. However, being positive isn't the only thing that affects your attitude. You should also be grateful. Grateful for the chance to mold young minds, to share your passion, and that you have a job in a world where so many people don't. This attitude will affect the students and anyone else around you, so make a point of being grateful and coming to class ready to be happy.

Stay Kind, Yet Firm

Don't let your students walk all over you. Students, particularly in the first few weeks of school, will test the limits. They want to know just how far they can push you and where the limits are. You can tell them, but they'll still need to test them. Often it takes just one student who pushes too far for the rest of the class to listen up and behave.

Your goal, as a teacher, is to focus on keeping order in the classroom, without losing your temper. But how do you do that without letting the students run amok?

The simplest way to do this is to let the student know you've seen them acting out, but will not tolerate it. Don't put the focus on the student, though. Instead, blend the correction into your lesson. For example, if you see Billy doodling and not paying attention in class, you might continue talking about fractions and say something like, "Not even one-third of this class will be permitted to ignore the teacher and doodle in their book like Billy." Then continue on with the lesson. It's a quiet, gentle poke to let the student know that you've seen them, but you're not willing to stop your lesson for their nonsense.

If the student continues to cause problems, or is disruptive, you can take them aside and explain that this is not acceptable behavior. Let them know that they are distracting the other students who need to learn and ask them what they think would be the best solution for this. You can also suggest that sitting elsewhere might help reduce the distraction and ask the student where they think they should sit. This puts the onus on the student to figure out a solution and shows that you trust them to make the right decision.

It's rarely necessary to raise your voice or be terribly strict with students, but being firm is a must. Do not let them walk all over you, but show kindness.

Be Caring

A caring teacher will have far more impact on students than one who is just focused on teaching. You're teaching children who have lives that affect their learning. If you show them that you care about their life outside of the classroom and their own personal interests, you'll soon have students who are focused and interested in your classes.

I've seen this happen again and again. A surly student finds themselves being treated gently despite their behavior and they start to wonder what's going on. They may lash out and test those boundaries, but when you keep showering them with caring attention, they eventually realize that it's real. That's when the breakthrough happens. I've seen so many students go from difficult to teach to fascinated by what is happening in class, because a teacher cared enough to talk to them and ask what was going on.

I find it particularly helpful to be caring outside of class. The student may feel that you're just being nice because you're paid to. However, when you see them in the hall and give them a fist bump or just say hi and ask how their test went, etc. they'll start to realize that you actually are sincere.

You can build loyalty in your students by genuinely caring about them. If you pay attention and take the time to connect, you'll be amazed at what can be accomplished.

Stay Calm

It's easy to blow your top when your students are acting up, but it's in everyone's best interest if you stay calm. That's easier said than done, however, since even the most patient of teachers has found themselves in a situation that is difficult to control their temper.

It is essential that you are the voice of reason in your classroom. No matter what your students do, you cannot lose your temper. So how do you stay calm? Try one of these techniques:

- Take deep breaths
- Close your eyes for a moment
- Walk to the window and look out
- Remind yourself of the good in the kids
- Count to 10
- Take a momentary break outside the classroom door
- Drink some cold water

Once you've collected yourself, you can deal with the situation. It's almost always beneficial to pause first.

Speak Clearly

While you can take this as a sign that you need to enunciate and speak very clearly, this is far more than just how you say the words. You also need to make sure you speak so that every student can understand. Some teachers have this knack from the beginning . . . others need to learn it. You have to figure out exactly how to explain the concepts in a way that your students will grasp them.

Sometimes this means relating the lesson to their lives in a way that might not normally be compared. I've found that students are far more likely to listen if you give them real-life situations where they might use the information you're presenting. However, if you can't explain the information in a way the student can take in, you have to try again. I have found that some concepts need to be explained in two or three different ways in order to ensure that all students have grasped them.

Do the Unexpected

Surprising your students can be a good way to get their attention and make sure they're focused. Imagine you're in the middle of an algebra lesson and it's dragging on. You're falling asleep, when suddenly, music fills the room and your teacher starts singing a song about algebra! Chances are, you wouldn't be falling asleep for much longer.

Of course, you don't have to sing and dance if that's not your thing, but you can surprise your students by doing things that they wouldn't expect. Taking the entire class outside to listen to the lecture under a tree, for example, will get them to wake up and pay attention.

When you do the unexpected, you break the mold. Your students tend to zone out because they think they know what is going on and they get bored. The same routine can become dull and cause complacency. So when you spice things up, it jars the brain and makes sure they're paying attention again.

Wondering what you can do to surprise your students?

Use technology. Instead of taking away their phones, request they bring them to class one day. Then have them use their phones for something related to the class. Not only is the turnabout interesting, but they'll be fascinated with the chance to actually use their phone in class. Another way to use technology is to video chat with a class on the other side of the country, or even an expert from another part of the world. Expand their horizons and introduce your students to some wonderful new ideas.

Put knowledge to use. Have students come up with a way to use what they've been learning in the real world. Not only will they have to use their skills, but they'll need to work as a team.

Flip the lesson. Tell students that they have to learn at home next time and come to class with their new knowledge. Or have the students explain the math or another lesson to you. It may surprise you how much they already know and students are often more willing to learn from other students.

Make it physical. Get your students out of their seats and have them actively participate in the class. In my math classes, I like to have races where I write a problem on the board and the students that come up with the answer move forward that many steps. If they're wrong (I reveal the answer), they have to go back that many steps. Simply moving will wake their brains up and get the students more interested.

Get silly. Wear a weird hat to class. Set up a strobe light. Do something really crazy and silly to startle your students out of their apathy and you have a surprising way to get them involved.

Bring the Humor

One of the best ways to defuse a potentially bad situation in a classroom is to make it funny. You can yell at a student to start behaving, or you can turn it into a joke. "Oh, I'm sorry to interrupt your nap, Johnny, but can I get your opinion on the 100 times tables?"

Making jokes can be particularly funny when you don't use them all the time. Students will find it unexpected (see the previous talent) and will be amused at the same time. No one expects a math teacher to crack jokes, for example, so when I pull one out of my hat, there's a burst of laughter after a moment of stunned silence. A class that laughs together learns together. Here are a few other ways you can bring humor into the classroom.

Post a cartoon. Find cartoons that suit your classroom and post one by the door each day. Students will enjoy having a chuckle as they come into the room each morning. You can bet some of them will start showing you cartoons they find, too.

Hold a joke day. I love to do this once or twice a year, where I challenge students to bring in their best math jokes. I give them a good week or two to find these jokes and they scour the internet in search of the funniest math jokes to use. Then we spend a whole class just telling jokes. It's hilarious. It's fun. And best of all, it creates an unstoppable bond between everyone in the class.

Laugh at yourself. If you mess up, go ahead and make a joke about yourself. Laugh it off. Students will follow your lead and laugh at their own mistakes. Even better, you can go ahead and make some mistakes or do something goofy on purpose to get them laughing. This is something to pull out from time to time to lighten the mood, something I find necessary in a math class!

Laughter alleviates tension in the classroom and you'll quickly become the favorite teacher in school. And let's face it, laughter is universal. Everyone will enjoy a good joke!

Be Consistent

Whatever methods of managing your classroom you select, you need to be consistent. The minute you waver, your students will pick up on this and will be more likely to challenge you. Start off strong and remain strong throughout the year. However, in order to be consistent, you need to have a plan right from the start. This can be adjusted, but you should present it to the students as an adjustment, and explain why you plan to make the change. This shows that everything is deliberate and you're not just making it up as you go.

Consistency will also earn respect. When a student flouts the rules and you reinforce them, everyone learns that you are serious about what you say.

Likewise, if you promise your students a pizza party if they work hard, you need to respect that promise and make sure you follow through. The consistency of what you say and what you do will show them that you mean what you say. It's a good way to earn their respect. This needs to be used with everything, no matter how small. If you make a commitment to a student, write it down and follow through.

If you are going to reward a student, be sure you are consistent in how you do so, every time you notice the behavior. You may need to make a note or do something to keep track of everything, but it's worth it.

Act with Respect

If you want your students to respect you, you need to respect them. It's easy to look at your students, particularly if they're very young, and think that they're just children. However, children are just as deserving of our respect as adults. They need to learn that it is the proper way to act.

Remember that you are showing the students how they should behave. Treat them with respect and you'll get respect in return.

Keep in mind that these are children, so it can take some time for them to learn what they need to do. Respect can be difficult if they have never had any reason to think of it before. They may not have seen this type of behavior modeled previously, so you'll need to teach them what it is.

Good ways to show respect to your students include:

- Offer them choices
- Greet everyone

- Don't raise your voice
- Listen when they speak
- Don't embarrass or humiliate them on purpose
- Correct their behavior calmly and subtly
- Do not engage in favoritism
- Stay consistent in the rules
- Speak to the student before going to the parent

You'll find that most students, when presented with respectful behavior, will respond by modeling it back to you. However, I've also found it useful to explain at the beginning of the year what I want from them and what being respectful means. This lets them know right off that they should be respectful in my classroom and then I model it for them.

Focus on Solutions

When you're a new teacher in particular, it's easy to go to the principal for every little misdemeanor. When a student acts out, you might find yourself getting frustrated and unsure of how to handle their behavior. What can you do to prevent things from getting out of control?

The simplest method is best. Focus on solutions. You are the leader in your classroom, so assert your authority and take care of problems in the classroom. It's fine to talk to other teachers about the problems you're having, with an eye to getting some advice, but you need to make sure that you are presenting yourself as the leader in the classroom.

There is nothing wrong with asking students for their ideas, as well. If a student cannot concentrate in class, you might take them aside and ask why they feel they're having trouble. From there, you can come up with a solution together. Instead of getting upset and frustrated with the student, look for a solution to the problem.

This helps you stay calm and it lets the class know that you will handle things in a reasonable manner. They may even start problem-solving on their own!

Model the Correct Behavior

If you want your students to behave a certain way, you need to show them how to behave. This works regardless of their age. To have respectful students, you need to respect them. If you want them to behave calmly in class, you need to be calm, as well. Students will quickly call you out if you ask them to do something but you do the opposite.

These are just a few of the skills you'll need as a teacher these days. Modern teachers need to model good behavior, act with respect, and be firm, yet kind. It can be a lot to balance, but it's well worth it to see the improvements in your classroom.

The Importance of Positive Reinforcement

Over the years, it has become increasingly evident that negative consequences do not have the desired outcome when dealing with children. Like most of us, kids will shy away from doing things that have negative results, if they think they'll get caught. However, it's been shown that positive reinforcement is far more likely to result in permanent behavioral changes.

What exactly is positive reinforcement? It is simply rewarding students when they do something well. Instead of punishing them, you focus on the good behavior and encouraging that. A simple example would be if one student is being noisy and disruptive by drumming on their desk, you might praise another student for paying attention and listening quietly. There's no shaming, no anger or punishment. The first student sees the second one is being praised for good behavior and begins to emulate it, in hopes of being praised, too. This is far more effective than sending the noisy student to stand in a corner or sending him to detention.

In order for positive reinforcement to work, you need more than just simple prizes. Kids love prizes, but you want to make sure that they understand why they are being rewarded. It's usually more effective to give them praise and compliments. After all, they crave recognition and when you give it to them, they'll be thrilled and continue to behave that way.

Make sure you speak to the student and tell them why you're proud of them. However, every student is different and some will be more resistant to actually seeking positive responses. Be patient.

How to Give Praise Correctly

There is a right and a wrong way to praise a child. If you just say, "Good job, Anika" the compliment is open to interpretation. What did you mean by it? Did you like the overall work? Did you like something specific? How can Anika repeat the job and impress you again?

This is the first thing to remember when you are using praise as a reward. You need to be **SPECIFIC**.

This means you pick out what you want to encourage and specify it. "Anika, you did a wonderful job organizing your art supplies." "Thank you for listening so well, Bobby." These are specific praises and tell the child exactly what they did that was worth the praise. They know which behavior to repeat.

You should also give praise frequently.

Avoid giving in to whining and other types of behavior that you do not want to encourage. This is positive reinforcement, but of a negative behavior. It is just as effective and you'll end up stuck with a bad behavior rather quickly.

Types of Positive Reinforcement

There are a number of ways to build on a good behavior and encourage it, beyond simple praise from the teacher. These include:

Natural reinforcement: When a child plays nicely or is kind to others, they are more likely to invite the child to work with them. Teachers do not really factor into this, but peers do, so it is an important method.

Tangible reinforcement: When you reward the child with an actual prize, this is considered a tangible way of reinforcing the behavior. In school, it's not usually a good idea to use an edible treat. Toys or small, fun prizes may work well, but can also cause problems if another student is never the recipient. Many teachers have found that awards or certificates are very useful for motivation, without the external problems of other prize types.

Social reinforcement: This type of reinforcement comes in the form of praise from peers, teachers, parents, and others who see that the child has worked hard. You may use words or smile and pat the child's shoulder, or write a note that praises them. These are very effective.

Point reinforcement: In this method, you give the child points or tickets for the correct behavior. The points aren't really worth anything, but once they collect a number of them, the child can turn in their points to receive a prize. Some teachers arrange kids into teams and the entire team earns points for everyone. You can even have the whole class earn points until they have enough for a group activity, such as a pizza party, etc.

Activity reinforcement: With this method of reinforcement, the student who has behaved well is permitted to do something fun, like play on their phone, take time on the computer, etc. You may even allow the student to pick a friend to join them, which increases the value of the reinforcement.

Which type of reinforcement should you use? That depends on the student. Most students have a preferred method of being rewarded. Start with praise and see how they react. If you find that some of the students are less than motivated with that, you can up the ante and offer a more important reward. The trick is to observe your kids and learn about them.

CHAPTER 4

YOUR FIRST DAYS OF SCHOOL

The beginning of the school year is the most essential part of the entire year. It's when you set the stage for the rest of your time with your class, so you need to lay out the ground rules and start in immediately. It's also important to get to know your students in these early days.

The Importance of the First Impression

The first day of school is when you meet your students. It's generally a time of getting to know them and explaining how your classroom will work. I highly recommend you stand at the door and greet each student and introduce yourself. They'll feel more confident walking in and will know who you are from the first moment.

That first impression is so important when it comes to students. You need to make sure that you are ready to connect with them and show them who you are. Start with the greeting and a big smile so they feel welcome. Your students should know that you're happy to see them and excited for the new year.

Once you've greeted everyone and they've all sat down, you can start in on the usual first day lessons. You'll want to introduce yourself again and give students an idea of who you are. You can also introduce the rules for the classroom and let them know exactly what you expect from them this year. This is a good time to introduce the concept of respect.

Take the time to show your students what respect means and how it should look in your classroom. Tell that that they need to respect themselves, you, the room, and other students. You can even roleplay a few scenarios to help them understand how to react in these situations.

You should also let your students know that mistakes are learning opportunities and that you are running a growth mindset classroom.

At the end of the day, stand by the door as your students file out and say goodbye to them, one by one. This leaves them with a good impression of you and of school on their first day.

Getting to Know Your Students

It's essential that you identify your students by name as quickly as possible. If you have their files ahead of time, you can memorize names and faces so you're able to greet each child with their name. That immediately makes them feel welcome. Otherwise, learn their names as quickly as possible once school has started. By the end of the first week, you should know their names and something about each student.

I also enjoy doing ice breaker activities that will help students get to know each other. It's a good way to have some fun on that first day and start building bonds between students and teacher. Need ideas for ice breaker activities? Here are a few that I've used:

Name Word Search: Create a word search that includes names for every student in the class. This is a good quiet activity to keep students busy while they're waiting for everyone to arrive.

Draw a Question: I write down a bunch of questions on tabs of paper and put them in a bag. Students take turns drawing a question and answering it. This tends to work best when we're all sitting in a circle.

Silent Dates: Tell the students to line up in order of birth month and day. There's just one catch . . . they can't talk. This can be a fun activity that results in a lot of laughter. Once they're lined up from January to December, have them do the opposite, December to January, but this time they can talk. I use this as a reminder that communication helps us complete tasks faster.

Time Capsule: Create a time capsule for the end of the year. Your students can write to their future selves and leave a picture or item in a box, which you then seal until the last day of the year.

Two Truths and a Lie. Have each student write down three "facts" about themselves. These should include two true facts and one lie. Then each person takes turns reading their three lines and students guess which is a lie.

Group Up: Have students form groups as quickly as possible, based on things you call out. For example, "shirt color" will send all students into groups of the same shirt color. You can also make them group up according to less obvious things like birth month, favorite food, favorite color, etc.

Any fun game that requires students to talk to each other will help them get to know each other.

Tips for Getting to Know Your Students

Something I learned from another teacher years ago is to assign students a special assignment on their first day in class. They have until the end of the week to write me a letter that tells me about them. I ask them to write down the most important thing I should know as a teacher, as well as anything else they want to tell me about their family, hobbies, any animals they might have, and their overall feeling about school. You would be surprised at how much information these letters can give you. It's also a great way to learn about how the student feels about your class. For example, many of the letters I'm handed tell me that Math is a terrible subject and they dislike it immensely. That immediately gives me a list of students who will need a bit of extra help.

Once you know what your students are interested in, you can incorporate that into your lessons. There's no rule that says every kid has to do the same exact problems. I've set it up so that the kids who are interested in business had to work on math problems that related to business, and the kids who wanted to be DJs or YouTubers worked with numbers dealing with those careers. The interest and focus were incredible, because they were working on something that actually mattered to them. Everyone learns best when they're interested, so it makes sense to take a little extra time to tailor the information to their needs.

Another good idea is to ask the parents to write you a letter. Ask them to tell you about their child. You'll find that they explain everything from emotional turmoil to attitude issues and problems that the child has had in school. From there, you can learn how parents handle things at home or how they wish things were handled at school. It's a great first step in starting to work with parents toward a common goal. It's also an excellent method of learning more about your students.

Listening: The Most Valuable Skill

Listening to your students is the perfect way to model the behavior you want from them and never is this more important than during the first few days of school. As your students get used to the new classroom, they'll tell you things and you need to make sure you listen and remember. I like to take notes on what students tell me and go over them at the end of the day. You never know when you might pick up on something that might be important.

Be an active listener. For smaller children, get down to their level. You should make eye contact with the student as they speak and nod as they talk. You can ask to follow up questions, as well, which will let them know you're genuinely interested in what they're saying.

Make listening a foundation of your classroom and your students will learn to listen to you when you speak, as well.

Mistakes to Avoid at All Costs

In general, you can recover from most mistakes you make in your first days as a teacher. However, if you mess up certain things, you'll find yourself fighting a losing battle for the rest of the school year. Here are some of the mistakes you really need to avoid at all costs:

Not Being Predictable

You can surprise your students sometimes, but if they have no idea what to expect from one day to the next, they'll be harder to control. The uncertainty causes problems and restlessness, because they never know what is going to happen. I highly suggest creating a classroom schedule so students know exactly what will happen over the next several days. If you can do similar activities on the same days each week, they'll feel more confident, knowing what is going to happen.

Not Making Your Expectations Clear

You should share what your expectations of the students are on the first day. Then make sure you stick to them. You have to give them something to work toward, so ensure they know what they are supposed to do. You can write the expectations out ahead of time so you can refer back to them as needed.

Making Too Many Rules

You don't need a lot of rules in a classroom. What is your main point of being in that room? To teach. What do the students need to be doing? Learning. The rules you make should be focused around those simple goals. For example, you might encourage students to "Be respectful" and "Be on time." Some teachers include, "Don't be a brat/stupid." However, everything really falls under being respectful. The fewer rules there are, the easier it is to enforce them. You can simply ask students if they think their behavior is respectful and remind them of the rule.

Not Engaging Them Immediately

Do you have downtime when students first enter the class? That's a surefire way to lose them right out of the gate. When students don't have anything specific to do upon entering the classroom, they start to talk, fidget, and fool around. In a few minutes, they're out of control and it can be very difficult to get them to quiet down again. Instead, make sure you have something for them to focus on as they enter. This could be a riddle on the board, or an invitation to create something. It will be far easier to get back on track this way.

Waiting to Reward or Discipline

When a child does something right at the beginning of class and you wait to reward them until the end, you'll find that the reward is not nearly as effective. The same goes for discipline. You need to acknowledge and deal with the issue immediately so students know you won't forget it or so they don't get further out of control.

Droning On for Too Long

Your lessons should be broken into sections. Students can only focus for up to 10 minutes at a time, so if you're talking for 50 minutes, they're going to zone out long before you finish. It's essential that you focus and break up the lesson, then involve them in activities to reinforce what they've just learned. This will keep their attention far better than teaching for a full hour, particularly on a difficult topic.

Being Too Nice

As a teacher, you probably want your students to like you and that's fine. However, you are there as a teacher, not a friend, so remember to be firm first. Again, keep the objective in mind. You're there to teach and they are there to learn. Is what you're doing conducive to those objectives? Don't let students walk all over you just because you want to be nice to them and have them treat you as a friend. They will respect you more if you know when to be firm.

Avoid making these mistakes and you'll find your school year goes much smoother.

CHAPTER 5

SET YOUR RULES, ROUTINES, AND PROCEDURES

An orderly classroom will only work out if you manage it properly. You need to start the year out on the right foot by setting up your routines and rules. I always encourage teachers to do this before the first day of school. You really want to have everything set up and ready so you can explain it all to the students when they arrive in your classroom.

Once you've set up your routines and procedures, you need to be consistent. Don't forget, the kids will test you and will try to check and see if they can push your limits. Be consistent, be firm, and insist things are done correctly right from the start. You don't want to give them any leeway in the beginning, because that will only lead to chaos later on.

Develop Your Routines

A routine is something you do every day. It's particularly useful in the classroom, because students know what to expect. For example, if you teach younger grades and cover all topics, you should create a routine that the students can count on. This might be starting out with a puzzle, then doing English, Science, having lunch and then moving on to Math, Reading, and Social Studies.

For most students, it's reassuring to know exactly what to expect. When they know what is coming, they can adjust to the changes and anticipate the next step in their day. You can also help them move from one part of the routine to the next by providing a five-minute warning. This will prevent any meltdowns that might occur when switching from one activity to the next. The signal can be a buzzer, you simply telling the students that they have five minutes, or something else. I've used a cowbell effectively in my classroom, but perhaps the best instrument I ever tried was a rainstick. These provide a gentle, soothing sound that my students seemed to appreciate and it was a great five-minute warning. I would then turn it over when the five minutes were up so they could move on to the next activity.

You will also want to let students know what is coming up. I do this with a calendar on the wall, but many teachers enjoy using an online calendar like Google Calendar to share the classroom schedule. Students can see at a glance what is going to occur in the month and can prepare for the changes.

Set Up Your Rules

It's easiest to manage your classroom if you keep the rules of the class to a minimum. It's easy to make a rule about every single behavior, from drinking water to talking with a friend. Anyone can do this, but it's also very limiting, because if you forget to include one thing in the rules, the kids will take advantage of this.

It's also very difficult to enforce rules when you have fifty of them. There are simply too many for students to remember. They can't follow the rules if they don't remember them all.

The trick is to keep things very, very simple. Don't have more than 2-3 rules, depending on what you need for your classroom. However, you should make these fairly broad. For example:

- Give Respect
- Don't Be a Brat
- Show Up On Time

Under respect, you can classify just about everything. If a student kicks another student's chair, you can ask if that's a respectful thing to do. If a child sasses you, again, it's about respect. Explain early on that your classroom runs on respect and you expect them to respect you, each other, and the items in the classroom.

Create Your Procedures

The procedures in your classroom should be there to help alleviate stress for both teachers and students. If you've ever struggled to get the class going or to prevent chaos at the end of class, then you need a procedure for these times. In fact, there are a few points that require a set procedure to ensure that you maximize your teaching time and the students have an effective learning space.

Starting Your Class On Time

It is essential that you be there before the class starts and you should expect your students to arrive on time, too. Greeting your students at the door is a good way to start the class off on the right foot. It can be as simple as saying good morning or simply giving a high five. The idea here is that it creates a positive vibe right from the start and you can remind them that class starts in so many minutes.

It's also helpful to engage students immediately as they enter the classroom, so you don't lose them to chatter and play while you're greeting everyone else. A journal prompt on the board or a puzzle on their desk can be a good way to keep them busy before you actually begin class. If they're busy as soon as they sit down at their desks, they have less time to goof off or cause trouble.

Lining Up

You may have a number of times when you want students to line up, so set up a procedure for this immediately. Students should learn that they need to take any necessary items with them (depending on the reason for lining up) and face the front of the line. They should not touch anyone else or talk and need to watch where they are going.

If students are leaving the classroom when they line up, they should be aware that they need to quietly get up and put their chair in its place before they move to the line. It should always be orderly.

This procedure is useful in so many places. I have used it when dismissing my class, while waiting for the bus on a field trip, or at a sports event. Anytime you need your students calm and orderly, you should be able to call out to them to line up and immediately see results.

Bathroom Excuses

Of course, you'll have students who need to use the bathroom during class, but this can be very disruptive to the rest of the class if you aren't careful. Giving permission in the middle of your lecture causes you to stop and interrupts the lesson for everyone. Instead of stopping your lecture, I suggest having a specific procedure in place that will control bathroom breaks without involving you.

For example, in my classroom, there is a single bathroom pass that I hang by the door. It's large enough to be noticeable, but there is only one. That means that when a student needs to go to the bathroom, they take the pass with them and hang it up again at the end of their trip. This limits the number of students that can go out at one time (no giggle sessions in the bathroom!) and frees me up to teach. It also allows students to control their own permissions, which is a big part of respect in the classroom.

Asking for Help

From time to time, a student may need your help in the classroom. How they ask for this help should be laid out in your procedures. Encourage students to ask their classmates for help, particularly if they are working at a table or in a group. Then, if they can't get help there, they should raise their hand or give whatever signal you choose to have them give you.

From there, you can go and help the student with what they need. It's a good idea to check if anyone else needs help, as well, since there may be a topic you didn't cover well enough and needs going over again.

It's also important to have a procedure for asking questions. You can ask students to raise their hand, or write the questions down to ask during a designated question period. The choice is yours, but whatever you select, be sure that you are consistent with it.

Handing in Work

When assignments are due to be handed in, you need to make sure your students follow protocol for handing them in. First, before anything, they should look at the paper and ensure they didn't miss anything. Their name should be at the top of the paper. From there, they should hand in the paper the way you have requested.

For many teachers, having a bin on their desk that is specifically for finished assignments is the most efficient method of receiving them. I keep a bin for this on my desk, which allows students to turn in their assignments while I am busy with other things, such as tutoring another student. It really saves time and you don't have to worry about papers sliding onto the floor.

Leaving the Classroom

Every classroom needs a procedure for leaving class. Without it, you end up with chaos whenever the bell rings. It's in your best interest to avoid this, so make sure you have a procedure that you can teach the kids. Ideally, they will put everything away and clean their desk area if needed (at the end of the day, for example). Then they should line up at a specific place, leading to the door. I like to put a line on my classroom floor to indicate the start of the line. When everyone is in the line and quiet, I give them the okay to leave and they neatly file out of the room.

This procedure makes life much simpler for the teacher. You'll be able to calmly dismiss your class and have them listen. If you have any last-minute announcements, having everyone quietly lined up is a great time to let them know.

How to Teach Your Routines to the Students

Now that you have everything organized and laid out, how do you get the students to follow what you've developed? The trick is to start right in on the first day. Make sure that you clearly explain everything and how it works. This is fairly simple the first day, since the kids will tend to listen.

I find it helpful to put up charts or posters with the most important information. Then, if any student "forgets" what they're supposed to do, you can point to the poster to remind them. Make sure to gently correct them if they do something off routine or try to skip a step in your procedures. It's essential that they follow them. You don't need to punish the student for mixing up a routine, just stop them and correct.

Correcting Improper Behavior

If your students are not doing as they're supposed to, for example, if they aren't lining up at the door to leave, like you told them to do, you need to correct this behavior immediately. A very effective method is to simply stand in silence and stare at them. After a minute, they'll realize that they're not being dismissed and will start to look at you. Once you have their attention, ask everyone to return to their seats. Ask why they were not dismissed and at least one student will probably tell you why you had to start over.

Let the students know that you're going to try again and remind them of the correct procedure. They should follow the correct procedure this time, but if they don't, you can guide them.

Remember, students who don't follow the procedures and routines need to be re-taught, rather than punished. This is keeping with the positive reinforcement concept and will help students behave better in the long run. However, you need to have patience. Some students have never had this kind of structure in their lives and will not understand how to follow it. You'll need to repeat, model, and repeat the behavior that you require from them.

Some teachers feel this teaching is a waste of time. Others believe children should enter the classroom ready to follow routines already. Neither of these is true.

First, when you take the time necessary to teach each class of students how to follow your procedures and routines, you save time down the road. Think about how much time you lose if you have to keep trying to calm a rowdy class. Even if your class starts just five minutes late because of lack of routine each morning and you lose another five minutes per class to disruptive students, that's 10 minutes a day. Nearly an hour every week. It all adds up.

When you teach your students to respect each other and the routines in place, you end up with a self-running classroom within a few weeks. The students will file in and find their seats, then begin whatever work you've set out for them. They will be calm and productive and listen well. You begin to maximize the amount of time you have to teach, so it actually saves time to teach them the procedures and routines early on.

Second, many teachers do not use these methods in their classroom, so even if you're teaching a higher grade, you cannot assume they already know how to enter a classroom correctly or follow your specific routines. These do need to be taught. If your students come into class knowing how to handle a routine, all the better, but you should never assume that they do.

Once your students have learned to follow all the rules, routines, and procedures, you'll find that your classroom is a calm environment, ideal for teaching and learning.

CHAPTER 6

BUILDING A MEANINGFUL RELATIONSHIP WITH YOUR STUDENTS

When you get down to it, everything about managing your classroom has to do with building a relationship with your students. When you know your students and they know you and there is mutual respect and connection, they won't even want to misbehave. Any issues that arise will be easily dealt with and you'll find it far simpler to manage your classroom.

Like everything else you do with your students, building relationships needs to be something you do consistently. You can't be kind and asking your students about their evening one day and then be sullen and angry the next. You need to always make yourself available to build on those relationships and every day should be a step closer to the ideal teacher-student bond.

Some students will come into your class, already wary and ready to hate the class. I see this particularly often in my class, since I teach math. There are a lot of kids who detest math and automatically assume that they are going to hate my class and therefore, me, too. They're in for a surprise though!

I pride myself on developing relationships with all my students, regardless of how they feel about math. When they realize this, they are usually surprised. It's impressive how many kids associate their teacher with the subject they teach. With a little caring and time, you can prove any kid wrong, though.

Best Strategies for Improving Student Relationships

How can you really get to know your students in the classroom? The main thing is to take an interest in them. When they see that you genuinely care about them, they will be far more likely to talk with you and become friends. It's easier than you might think. Though they're kids, they're still human, so you just need to find some things in common.

From the first day, you should be collecting information on your students, or even before. Write notes to the parents, asking them to give you some insights. Ask your students about their lives. Get to know their favorite:

- Animal
- Color
- Food
- Place
- Activity
- Class

As you learn more about them, you'll find out that there are many interests you can use in the classroom. You'll also start to learn that your students require different teaching methods. You can begin to tailor the lessons to the different types of learners in your room.

Every student is different, but as you get to know them, you'll find that there's a solution to every problem. So if you have a troublesome student, it's really about getting to know them and finding out what makes them tick. From there, you can build their curiosity about the lessons and help engage them.

Create a Hang Out Space

When students come to school in the morning, where do they hang out? What if you make that space your own classroom? If your classroom is a comfortable spot to chill before class and just relax a bit, you have the opportunity to connect with students and see what is up in their life. A couple of bean bag chairs at the back of the room is perfect for encouraging kids to come chill in your room.

I also like to have some tea for my older students. I drink tea, so I have a little extra and they can drink tea and have a cookie while they're waiting for school to begin. It's not a big deal, but it just makes my classroom a bit more inviting. Then I can also grab a student who has been particularly troublesome and invite them to have a cup of tea and chat with me so we can maybe work through their problems.

Believe In Your Students

You, as a teacher, have a unique role to play in your students' lives. They look up to you and you can actually have a huge effect on how they see themselves. A single teacher telling a child they are stupid can have lasting consequences and we all know the horror stories. However, telling a child they are a hard worker and can accomplish anything will yield the opposite result. If you want to shape the leaders of tomorrow, you need to believe in them and make sure they know that you have high expectations.

It's your duty to help students believe in themselves and to feel strong and powerful. If a child has poor grades, sit down with them to figure out why. What did they not understand? Do you need to explain it in a different way? Let them know that you are there to help and that you know they're going to get it. It can be a very powerful thing to have an adult believe in you when you're still young.

Your students, when they respect you, will strive to reach your expectations, so if you expect a lot from them, they will rise to the occasion. Not only is this a good way to show them what they are capable of, but it can also help them learn far more than they ever thought they were capable of.

Be Empathetic

Your classroom should be a safe place for the students. When you make it a room where you get to be yourself and will be treated with respect. This can be accomplished by practicing empathy with everyone in the room. However, something you should do is encourage your students to treat each other with empathy, as well.

In your class, you need to celebrate everyone. You can do this by:

Celebrating their differences: Encourage your students to share their cultural heritage and their different interests. You can do this by having them do presentations on family traditions, hobbies, and other interests. It will help everyone enjoy learning something new and they can share their own interests.

Share their opinions: Students should have a chance to share their opinions in a respectful environment. You can do this by teaching them how to present their thoughts in a way that doesn't hurt other people. It's also a good time to share how to accept opinions that you don't agree with. I find it most useful to stage healthy debates where students can present their opinion and why they think that way, while others can offer an opposing view.

Support each other: When a student is going through a difficult time, you can help support them, but nothing is more helpful than having a whole classroom of peers supporting them. Teach your students to help one another and to ask if someone needs help when they see them struggling. If you can convey this in your classroom, you will ensure that they have a brighter future ahead of them. Your students will be far more respectful to each other and to you, as well.

Create an Interesting Learning Environment

Students learn best in an exciting, energetic environment. It makes sense. After all, if you are sitting in a lecture and the professor is droning on and on, it can be very dull and you're more likely to fall asleep than to learn. The same goes for your students.

If you want to build strong bonds with your students, you should make learning interesting. This means you can't just present the information. You need to be engaging and exciting. When you're passionate about a topic, you can find ways to convey that to your students. I know that math isn't a terribly compelling topic for most kids, but I find ways to make it relatable for everyone in my class. That's what you should be doing, no matter what subject you teach.

Every morning, when you greet your students, be uplifting and happy. They'll immediately feel better about coming to class and will be more likely to perform better.

Build Trust

A good relationship is all about trust. Do your students trust you? Do you trust them?

Once your students trust you, they'll be more willing to talk to you and will happily share their lives with you. This is good, because it will allow them to open up with you.

The simplest way to build trust is to open up to your students yourself. Be honest with them. They should know that you will always be truthful and talk to them. Share information about yourself and they'll be more inclined to talk to you about their lives, as well.

It may be tempting to separate your life and school, but in order to build a true relationship with your students, you need to share with them.

Use their names: It is very, very important that you use students' names and learn to pronounce them correctly. Never give children a nickname unless they ask you to call them by that. When they come in each morning, you can greet them by name and they'll feel valued and cared for.

Share their accomplishments: I love to take photos of my students when they're giving presentations or working on projects together. Then I hang these up on the bulletin board. Kids love to see pictures of themselves and it makes them feel valued, as well. This is a very simple way to appreciate them and build up those relationships.

Listen to them share: Your students need caring adults in their lives. If you listen to them, they'll learn to trust you and to share everything with you. You have a very unique opportunity when it comes to the children in your classroom. When you listen to the students talk, you'll be surprised at how much they'll share. I love talking to my students, even when it has nothing to do with the classwork.

Make Every Student Feel Special

A great way to build those relationships with your students is to make them feel chosen and special. You can do this in a number of ways, but basically, you need to treat each student as an individual.

Make a point of speaking to each student individually at some point during the day. This can be challenging, but it's worth making the effort. Even if it's just a quick check-in, you will make their day. Try to remember important events, like siblings being born, parents going on trips, etc. so you can inquire about them. The fact that you remembered will help cement your interest in the child's mind and that can help create a bond.

Joking with the students is a fun way to create bonds, as well. They'll love to share their favorite jokes with you, too. Try to have a new one every few days to share with them and watch them light up when they have something new to tell you.

Another way to really make a connection and help your students feel special is to share a meal with them. You can arrange for a handful of children to eat with you each month, switching it up so everyone gets a chance to share a meal with you. There's nothing like eating together to really make you open up and get to know someone. It works well with students, as well as friends and it really makes them feel special.

Create a Stimulating Environment

You're the one who sets the tone in the classroom, so take the time to make it really work and feel like a place that kids can come to and be themselves.

Demonstrate and Guide

As a teacher, you'll find that guiding your students is easiest if you model or demonstrate the desired behavior. If you want them to accept everyone in the class, make sure you accept everyone. If you want them to respect each other, show them exactly what that type of respect looks like and give them guidance so they can repeat it.

Depending on which grades you teach, you are with your students for a very large part of their day. If you can show them exactly how to accept others, respect each other, and to express their opinions civilly, you're going to have a huge impact on their lives. You may only have the students for a year, but you're going to have a chance to show them how to act like good, kind human beings. That cannot be underestimated.

Motivate and Reward

Students, like everyone, do best when they are motivated. It's hard to do your homework when you hate the class and know you're going to be chastised anyway. However, if there is some sort of motivation for trying hard and your teacher rewards you for doing your best, there is motivation.

I also like to motivate my students with real-world studies of how they can use what I teach them. This is particularly important in a subject like math, where it may seem ridiculous to learn algebra. I've had many students ask where they're going to use this type of math in their life. Without real reasons to learn, kids tend to give up easily. If it's hard and they don't understand how it can benefit them, they're just doing it to please teachers and parents. And that isn't always enough motivation.

Give your students a reason to learn and watch them take off. It can be helpful to have them do the scouting and investigate how the information they're learning now will help them in the future. Something else I always push is the fact that learning how to learn is a valuable skill that will serve them well throughout their lifetime.

Stimulate and Inspire

Your students probably have very different personalities and learning methods. Some will be very curious and seek out answers on their own. Others will tend to hang back and wait for you to tell them what to do. The idea here is to get them to start learning on their own and to stimulate and inspire them to follow their interests.

You can do this by providing invitations that let the students choose their path. How will they react if they come into the classroom and find a huge stack of number blocks on their desk? I've tried this. Some students sat down and waited for me to explain. Others started to play with the blocks immediately. Some lined them up in numerical order, and others started to make math problems with them. It was a fascinating experiment that showed me more about how their minds work.

CHAPTER 7

HOW TO DEVELOP A POSITIVE LEARNING ENVIRONMENT

Studies have shown that students learn best in an environment that is conducive to learning, or a positive learning environment. Remember that your students come from many different backgrounds and some may not have the best home life. They need a place where they can be certain they are safe and cared for. No matter their age, this is an important part of growing and learning.

Only when a child feels safe can they actually learn. However, you can also create a positive environment for them to acquire knowledge that will enhance how much they learn. Don't just provide a safe haven for the child, be sure that they are given the best opportunity possible to learn and grow.

Creating a positive environment for your students begins before they even walk in the door on the first day of school. The space you create should feel warm and inviting, so they know immediately upon entering that they are safe and can learn here.

There are many other ways to build a positive learning environment, but the key here is engagement. You want to engage your students and involve them in their learning. If they are willing participants, they will learn faster and more solidly than if they are simply forced to sit and listen.

Easy Ways to Engage Your Students

Wondering how you can get your students actually participating in the classroom studies? You may need to try a few different things in order to capture the attention and interest of all the students in your classroom. Experiment with different ideas and see what sparks interest in each of them. As you get to know your students better, you will be able to gauge their reactions to various types of activities.

Focus On Their Needs

What do your students need? I'm a firm believer that the student has to come first if you want them to actually learn. Find out what they need and then present the material in a way that works for them. Obviously this can be challenging if you have a lot of kids in the class, but it's worth it.

If you have students who learn best by doing, you can get them to actively participate in the class by writing on the board for you, holding your props, or doing other things that will aid you in teaching the class, but give them the movement they need.

Keep in mind that students who are hungry, scared, or sad will also have special needs when it comes to class. Try to address these (privately, of course) before you expect the student to learn properly. By addressing the needs of the students before you try to teach them, you'll end up with a much more engaged classroom.

Make Use of Technology

Need to get a point across in today's classroom? Try a meme. You can even make your own meme if you really want to get ambitious, but there are plenty out there that work very well. One fun activity I enjoy is giving students a blank meme and asking them to fill it in, making it relevant to math class. The funniest results are hung on the bulletin board where we can all laugh at them for the rest of the week.

Memes aren't the only way to use technology, though. You can set up a WhatsApp group for your class and be a regular participant in it. You can create a slideshow of your summer vacation and show students what you have been up to. Or you could create an Instagram (private, of course) for your students and post images of them doing their assorted activities. It's a high-tech world now and students are more familiar with smartphones than calculators, so make use of that.

One of my most successful assignments was asking students to design an app. They paired off and brainstormed ideas. You may think this is an odd assignment for a math class, but I tied it into math by having them work out how much they could sell the app for, if they would include in-app purchases, and how much they'd spend on marketing and development. The students loved it. It spoke to their interest in electronics and tech and they all had great ideas. It was fun to see the amount of passion they brought to the project, because it was something they were actually interested in.

Use Gamification

Anything can be turned into a game if you try, even pre-calculus. Turning learning into a game is a fun way to make it interesting and kids will immediately be more interested. I personally like to use games that require moving around, so they are getting out of their seats and are fully engaged with each other. One excellent way to do this is to create an escape room scenario and have the students try to escape before the class is over. You can adjust this to any class subject and have them go through the scenario using what they've learned.

Other fun ways to gamify learning include:

Memory: Create memory cards that students can flip, with pertinent facts on them. Alternatively, you could just call on students to randomly tell you the answers to questions you ask, much like a pop quiz.

Basta: Pick a letter from a hat and have students write down five words from a specific subject that start with that letter in one minute. You could also create a list of categories that they need to fill out. For example, in Geography, you might have them write a city, state, country, and building that start with the chosen letter. Have students read out their answers and give them a point for every blank they filled in.

Trivia Race: Divide the class into two teams and mark squares on the blackboard. You will read out questions and the teams answer as quickly as possible, moving their marker up the board as they get the answer correct. This is actually very much like a pop quiz, but so much more fun.

These are just a few ideas to get you started. You can turn anything into a game, if you really want to. If you're stuck for ideas, just ask your students for a few ideas. Chances are, they'll be thrilled to help you out, especially if it means they get to design and manage a game that their fellow students will be able to play.

Tell Stories

Who doesn't love a good anecdote? Humans were meant for storytelling. It was one of our earliest forms of teaching and learning and it is still ingrained in us today. Next time you're about to teach a classroom something, dig up a story about the person who invented it or something similar. Talking about the position of the sun and planets? Why not tell them a story about Galileo?

As adults, we appreciate a good story. So do kids, in fact, they may even enjoy it more than we do. Take the time to find anecdotes about some of the most boring subjects you have and watch the interest immediately spark. It only needs to be tangentially related to the actual lesson, so get creative.

Use Props

Blackboards and posters are useful and certainly have their place in the classroom, but have you ever considered using other items in your lessons? Props can make the words you're speaking far more interesting. I knew a teacher once who actually used a puppet to teach health class. She told her students she had a guest speaker and pulled out the puppet. Of course, it got a lot of laughs, but since it was new and unique, it certainly did the trick.

In math class, I've used everything from plastic models to Lego and sugar cubes. Look around you and see what you can use to illustrate your lessons. Just having something in your hands will immediately peak the kids' interests and have them curious about what you're going to teach. That curiosity is what you want to encourage and build on. That's what gets kids engaged.

Add Some Movement

School is long and tedious for many kids, but when a child is naturally inclined to run and jump all day, it can be sheer torture. That's why I love to get my students moving. They appreciate it and listen far better in my classes. How can you add movement to your class without losing control of the class?

Give them a task. They'll need to do something specific, like talk to a classmate or find something in the classroom. When the student is on a mission, they won't be causing trouble, but they will be moving around. This helps release some of the pent-up energy they might have.

Have a stretching moment. If I notice that my students are starting to drift off or lose focus, I call them all to stand up and move to the side of their desks. Then we do some stretches, jog in place, and generally get the blood flowing. They'll wake up and be more involved in the class after that.

Make interaction active. If you ask a question in your lesson, ask all the students who know the answer to stand up and touch their toes. The next time you ask, have them spin three times in place. These simple ways of including movement in the lesson will help keep them on their toes and paying attention.

You can always find ways to make movement part of your classroom. The students will love it and will eagerly participate. Even if they act reluctant, they are probably enjoying the opportunity to get out of their seats and enjoy a little movement.

Make Your Classroom Interactive

Forget standing in front of your students and talking to them as a method of teaching. While you can do that and many teachers still do, there's so much more you can do that will actively engage students.

Getting students to give presentations is a good way to build their confidence and encourage them to learn on their own, but you can take it a step further and have kids collaborate on a bigger project. Something I've done is hand out individual sheets for kids to color in with just two colors, blue and red. They take these home and color them and when they come to class, they have to put their individual pieces together to form a picture. This is then taped together and we hang it on the wall and incorporate it into the lesson. The students are immediately invested in the class, because they have actively participated in creating part of it.

Technology also makes it easy for students to interact in the class. You can use online quizzes or surveys to get them involved in the topic and then present them with the actual lesson. Or you can use Skype to talk to an expert or even another classroom across the country or world. Use your imagination to expand the ways your students can use tech to reach out and interact.

Another good technique is two facts and a lie. Write down two facts on the board, but then include a lie in there, as well. This can all relate to the lesson. Students need to call out the facts and just the facts. If you have a few of these lined up, it can be a fun game for the class . . . they won't even notice they're learning.

Encourage Peer Learning

You have a very valuable resource in your classroom and that is the students themselves. They are right there and all you need to do is start working with them.

Peer to peer learning is very powerful. After all, who understands a fellow student better? You can do this in many ways, but a quick and easy method is just to put a problem on the board and let the kids start solving it. Give them a time limit. At the end, you can have the ones who got the correct answer team up with the ones who did not solve the problem or got it wrong. Then the students who understood the problem can explain how they arrived at that particular solution. Not only does it reinforce what the student knows, it also gets them to explain it in a way that other students can understand.

Another option is to have each student study a certain part of the topic and present their findings. Together, they all have the full lesson, presented piece by piece, student by student.

Ask a Lot of Questions

Your students probably know more than you give them credit for, so include them in the lessons. Ask questions before you teach something new and see if anyone is able to explain it. You can then use that student as part of your lesson, including them. The other students will instantly be more interested because their peer is involved and they can see that this is something anyone can know about, even kids their age.

I also like to ask questions that get them thinking. For example, if you ask a group of third graders something like "What is 10 times three?" They might be confused. So you then ask, "What is 10 plus 10 plus 10?" Someone will probably answer. You can then explain that multiplication is just a simpler way of saying a number plus itself many times. Since they started thinking for themselves instead of you just telling them everything, it gets their minds working and they're more likely to understand the lesson.

Wherever possible, ask questions and get your students thinking. Even if they don't come up with the answer, they're working on it and are engaged in the lesson.

Creating an engaging classroom requires you to think outside the box a bit. You'll find that kids are more interested in learning when they have the chance to actually participate in their education. Make your classes more engaging and you'll have students who learn better.

CHAPTER 8

DEALING WITH DIFFICULT STUDENTS

Every teacher has to deal with difficult students from time to time. These are students who have difficulties that make them harder to deal with, but it doesn't always mean they are bad kids. In fact, they might be really awesome kids, but they have issues with certain things.

All students will benefit from having you believe in them. Your expectations mean something to them, even if they don't let that show. Remember that most troublesome students have already been told that they are stupid or problematic. These words sink into their heads and they become their own self-talk.

If your student has always been considered difficult or if they are being treated as a difficult child at home, they will probably just go ahead and live up to that. After all, what's the point in behaving when no one cares?

You making a point of treating the troublesome student as if they were worth something is the best thing you can do. Reverse the negative self-talk, whatever it is and tell them that you believe in them.

Implement a System for Success

Regardless of the type of difficult student you're dealing with, you will find that setting them up for success is essential. They need to feel that rush that comes with accomplishing something. Since it can be problematic to do individual rewards, particularly if a student refuses to even try, I like to do class challenges. This way, everyone contributes, no matter how small, and they all get rewarded. Even the tough students can enjoy the reward.

Challenges can be anything from doing classroom chores each day and ticking them off, to acts of kindness and good behavior that earn them points. When they get enough points, they are rewarded.

Rewards can include:

- Free period
- Pizza party
- Outdoor class
- Movie
- Game day
- No weekend homework

Come up with something that your students really enjoy and you'll see some drastic improvements in behavior. I find it particularly helpful to surprise the difficult student by making them part of the classroom success. You may have to dig to find it, but one small good behavior and you can congratulate them for adding a point to the roster. They then begin to feel ownership of the challenge and will often start participating on purpose.

Have a Lot of Fun

Fun activities will draw most people out of their corner and students can get to know each other over a craft or game. While you can't always use these methods in your classroom, incorporating fun into your lessons will help students bond and enjoy the lessons. Eventually, you'll find that they start to bond a little more with you and with their classmates.

Types of Difficult Students

There are a number of different types of difficult students, and they all require their own special handling, so let's take a look at the various ones you might encounter.

Shy Students

These students aren't causing problems, in fact, they're probably hiding from them. Your shy students may not speak even when called on and will never, ever volunteer information. They're hard to draw out, because they are so uncomfortable in a group. Over the years, I've learned a few things about shy students.

Talk to them one on one. They are far more comfortable one on one, so make a point of talking to them individually. You'll often find that they are funny and chatty when you get them alone.

Never let your students pick their seats. This is a good way to ensure best friends sit together and others are marginalized. Sit your shy students in front, to ensure you can interact with them. If they are very uncomfortable with this, you may need to put them in front, but to the side, so they can still feel safe. Remember that you want to work with them, not humiliate them.

Call on them, even if they don't volunteer. Shy students aren't going to raise their hands, but you should call on them sometimes anyway, especially if you know they know the answer. Don't always rely on the hand-raising method to get your answers, since only certain students will do this.

Assign them an extrovert. You'll have extroverts in your class, as well, so when teaming students up, be sure to put an introvert with at least one extrovert. They'll encourage the shy student to come out of their shell. This is all part of having an inclusive classroom, too. Everyone should be able to get along with everyone else.

Be patient. It takes time for shy students to come out of their shell and start to feel accepted in the classroom. When you notice that they are making a move to participate, acknowledge it and be sure to encourage them. It could take months for these students to really start participating on their own, but if you are patient, it will happen.

Shy students may be naturally quiet, or they may be unsure of themselves. You can gradually build them up and help them become more outgoing by providing a safe environment to step out.

Slow Learners

You may have students with learning disabilities in your class and they will have their own needs. However, some students don't necessarily have a learning disability, they just learn

83

slower than everyone else in the class. This can be very frustrating for everyone, including the student. After all, the class moves at the pace of the slowest student, or leaves them behind. So how do you handle the student that simply can't keep up?

Repeat the learning points. For each major learning point, you should say it and then rephrase it to give the slower student a chance to pick it up. By rephrasing, you also ensure any students who don't understand the first way you said it will get the second. This is useful in any classroom setting.

Ask other students questions. The slower learner will hear the answers the other students give, so you are not only engaging the other students, but you're also providing an option for this student to think about what is being taught and hear how another student explains it.

Use audio and visual props. Not everyone learns simply by hearing a teacher talk. Adding in video or using technology to create a learning opportunity can help those visual and audio learners understand the lesson faster. It's a good idea to assess the learning styles in your classroom and be sure to address them all.

Stick to the main points. Summarizing a lesson at the end is a good way to help all your students, but it will be particularly useful for those who cannot manage too many details. Give them the "too long, didn't read" version at the end of each class.

Offer study guides for tests. All your students will appreciate knowing what information they should focus on in order to prepare for the test. However, for the slower learners who cannot process as much information, knowing where to direct their energy will be particularly helpful.

Provide real-life scenarios. Students need to know why they're learning a specific concept, so go ahead and give them a real-life scenario where they could use the information you're teaching. This will give them more reason to focus on the lesson. You need to make the lessons relevant so they'll be interested in learning. The more interest they have, the more likely they are to actually learn.

Review the basics. If you have a slow learning in your class who is really having difficulty, check that they understand the basics. I've seen this happen many times, where a student never fully grasped the basics of multiplication and division, so they are having trouble with algebra. You may need to revisit the base information in order to teach them the more advanced version.

Focus on their strengths. In group projects or in individual projects, make sure you include some activities that the slower learners are very good at. They'll feel successful when they can do something better than others. Often, a child who is slow to read will be great at sports or art. Play to their strengths to give them a confidence boost.

If you find it difficult to teach slow learners, just remember that they will need to hear the same information multiple times. They also learn faster when they have the opportunity to apply the lesson to their real life.

ADHD and Hyperactive Students

These kids aren't trying to make trouble, they just can't help but move. They probably learn best if they're moving, fidgeting, or actively taking part in the lesson and if they're not, then you may find them disruptive. Whether or not a student has been diagnosed with ADHD, you can help them focus more with a few specific methods.

Let them move. Movement is part of learning for these students and if you force them to sit still, they probably won't remember a bit of the lesson. Wiggle chairs, exercise balls, and standing desks are just a few of the options that can help them learn. Don't complain if they jiggle a leg and twist and turn in their seat. You may find that it distracts other students, so set your hyper student on an edge of the class where they can move without distracting anyone.

Keep things simple. When speaking to a hyperactive child, you should keep it short and sweet. They may not be able to focus on your words for long, so make sure you keep your sentences short. Make it easy to understand and break it into bite-sized pieces.

Get them to repeat. It can be helpful to have the student repeat what you just said, so you know they heard you. If they can't, repeat it again. Keep in mind that it isn't always helpful to force the student to sit still and look at you. When you do this, the hyperactive mind is busy thinking about moving and not absorbing the information you're sharing.

Check-in with them. Your student may find it frustrating to try and stay quiet and still over time. It's a good idea to check on them and determine if they need a short break. Just the fact that you're checking in will help them feel more accepted.

Hyper and ADHD students will require a little extra care, but when you treat them right and respect their need to move, you'll find that they can actually learn fairly rapidly.

Trouble Makers

The very first thing you need to do with a trouble maker is get to know them. Make it your mission to figure out how that child ticks and connect with them. It's hard when you feel annoyed or irritated on a regular basis with the student, but your attitude toward them should always be kind. Very few children are genuinely unlikeable when you break past that trouble-causing exterior. You can also try the following methods:

Be consistent. Troublesome students often need to repeat the exact same behavior and receive the consequences multiple times. You need to be consistent, to ensure they know exactly what is coming, every time they engage in that particular behavior.

Let them make choices. Every student will benefit from having a choice in how they study and learn, so go ahead and give this option to your troublemakers, too. The fact that you're trusting them to choose the right thing will help the student see you in a different light. They will feel more responsible and will hopefully start acting that way, too.

Don't interrupt the class for them. Often, students cause issues in class because they want attention. Even negative attention is something they will take, so they act out. It's best not to give them the attention they want. Do not stop your lesson or interrupt your class for them. Just keep talking and give a quick reprimand, included in the speech. For example, if you're talking about Isaac Newton, you might say, "Isaac was a bit of a daydreamer and he probably liked to interrupt people who were speaking, just like Jack over here." Then continue on. The student knows they have been seen, but they also learn that their behavior will not glean more attention.

Give a signal for a brain break. If your difficult student tends to cause problems during periods of intense concentration, develop a signal that lets them know, without interrupting the class, that you think they need to take a minute and count to 10.

Be trustworthy. Often, students who cause problems in the classroom have had a rough upbringing or are dealing with a lot in their personal lives. They may even be the victim of bullying. You never know what is going on, so make sure you give them the benefit of the doubt. You should also be trustworthy. It's possible they don't have any adults they can trust in their life, so give them the chance to know one. Fulfill your promises and make sure that you always do what you say, so the student realizes you are for real.

Focus on the relationship. Forget the classroom for a bit and work on just getting to know the student. Make a connection and the learning will follow. It's important to remember that our students are far more than just students in a classroom. They're people and they have their ups and downs, just like the rest of us.

Stay cool. When you're calm, kids can't get a reaction out of you and they eventually stop trying. It's also very helpful to just go up to the student who refuses to work and say to them, "So you're refusing to work? You want to be defiant? You're telling me that you are going to come to my classroom and not work? They often become very uncomfortable and will start doing the work.

Troublemakers can wreak havoc in your classroom, so it's in your best interest to figure out how to manage them quickly and effectively.

CHAPTER 9

MY FAVORITE CLASSROOM MANAGEMENT HACKS

Your classroom can either be a well-oiled machine or a space of chaos. Hopefully, it's already somewhat organized and runs well, but if it doesn't, these hacks will help you turn your classroom into a space that works as a learning environment. Your students will be attentive and listen correctly if you stick to these hacks.

Of course, you don't need to use all of these. I'm giving you the best ones I have in my arsenal and it's up to you to decide which methods you want to use in your classroom. There are plenty of ways to manage your classroom and none of them is the only way. Use what works best for you and for your students.

Classroom Management Hacks

Managing your classroom can be challenging, but there are always ways to make things easier. Here are a few of the hacks I use for managing my classroom and keeping it as a calm and positive learning environment.

Secret Symbol or Code Word

Do you have a student who is particularly disruptive, not because they mean to be, but because they just lose focus? I actually used this method with my son for when he was misbehaving. Instead of calling the child out, you talk with them privately and set up a secret symbol or a code word. For my son, that was "Sharkbait." Every time the student is acting out, you just give them the secret symbol or say the word. They know that they need to stop and focus. It's a very effective way to call a student out without actually embarrassing them. It also lets the student have a special bond with you. Do it with all your kids.

Scent Rewards

Before implementing this one, be sure your students don't have allergies to any of the ingredients in the lip balm you use. Select a fun smelling lip balm or chapstick and whenever you see a student doing a particularly good job at concentrating, put a dab on the back of their hand. They can then smell it as a reward for working hard. You can use this as a simple, yet surprisingly effective reward for any desirable behavior. Even better, change scents each month to create more interest.

Hand Signals

Are you tired of your students constantly asking permission to do things? While older students can follow instructions like our bathroom procedure mentioned earlier in this book, you may want to implement hand signals for your students. This can be as simple as a number symbol with your hand and it allows you to see which students need to sharpen a pencil, get a drink, or do something else. Create signals for anything that your students might ask and then require them to quietly sit in their seat and give you the signal. When you nod at them, they can go do whatever they're asking to do.

When you use hand signals, it's not necessary to interrupt the class constantly just to have a student ask for an extra tissue or a pencil. It's all done silently and you can give permission while you continue with your lesson.

Student-Teacher

If you have a problem with students asking you questions when you're trying to focus on another student or a small group of students, you can assign a student-teacher. This student should be one of your more responsible students. It's a special responsibility that brings a lot of prestige. You can give them a lanyard with a "student-teacher" badge and instruct all other students to ask their questions of the student teacher.

This method frees you up to focus on the kids who need your help and the student-teacher will be learning as they teach and answer questions. This method is implemented for lower grades, but I've actually found it useful even for higher grades.

Pick a Mystery Student

Draw a name from a hat and that student is your mystery student for the day. Keep an eye on them and see how well they behave throughout the day. At the end of the day, if they did well, you reveal who it was and give them a reward. Since students don't know who the mystery student is, they'll be more likely to watch their behavior, because it could be them! If you don't see the kind of behavior you want, don't tell them who the mystery student was, just tell the entire class that you would like to see better behavior from them.

Classroom Organization Hacks

Every classroom needs to be organized. If you can't find the items you want to use, it's going to be tough to teach. However, you should also have everything set up so that students can be as independent as possible, so you can empower them.

Die Cut Storage

When you have a lot of die cuts for your bulletin board, you can use a DVD case to store them. They'll stay organized and won't get bent, but you'll be able to quickly and easily find exactly what you need. You can organize them by bulletin board theme, in alphabetical order, or however you like.

Look Up Board

Curb the constant questions about what you're going to be doing in class next or when the test is by using a Look Up board. This is just a simple bulletin board where you post all upcoming information and any rules, consequences, etc. If your students are constantly asking about it, put it on the Look Up board so they can check for themselves.

Extra Supplies

Do your students come in with a lot of extra supplies that need to be stored? You can use a simple shoe organizer hanging on the door to manage their things. Add their names to each of the pockets and keep their items in their pockets.

Alternatively, you could use sets of plastic drawers to keep all those extra supplies in and just mark each item with the student's name.

Manipulatives

Baskets or desk caddies are ideal for storing manipulatives that you're going to be using all the time. If you have manipulatives that aren't used that often, you may prefer plastic drawers like those for craft supplies. This will keep everything nice and organized.

Student Papers

Your students will be turning in a lot of papers throughout the year, so keeping them organized is key. I like to use plastic boxes to prevent papers from sliding around and use a different color for each class. For example, Grade 6's put their papers in the blue box, Grade 7's in the green.

Another quick and easy option for managing the paperwork that belongs to each student is to use binder clips. Just add new sheets to the clip as the student completes them and then flip one loop up to hang on a peg on the wall. I use large binder clips so you can write the student's name on it.

Guest Teacher Binder

Nearly every teacher has a day or two when they can't get to school. On those days, your class will have a substitute or guest teacher binder. I like to have all the basic information for a new teacher compiled in here. This includes rules, procedures, and routines. They can see at a glance what is permitted and what is not.

You may also want to include a lesson plan that can be followed if they like, which is not specific to anything in particular in your class. It can be taught in the first weeks or later on in the year, but will help students review material.

Grading

Need to grade papers at home? If you're like most teachers, your work isn't finished when you leave the classroom. A good way to keep track of everything is to use an expandable folder that you can keep different classwork in and you'll be able to grade it at home. The various sections in the expandable envelope let you separate work by grade or class and you can easily work on just one section at a time.

Lesson Plans

If you develop your own lesson plans or are adding to the curriculum, you should keep it all in the cloud. I personally use Dropbox for all my lesson plans, but you can use whatever works for you. Keep a folder for each class and then divide those by date. Since they're in the cloud, you can access the information from anywhere, including your phone, laptop, or school computer.

Seasonal Decor

If you change the decorations in your room for the various seasons, you need to keep track of everything and make it super easy to grab what you need in a moment. Bins that can be labeled are perfect for this, especially since they come in multiple sizes. You can use whatever size you need to fit the decorations. For example, I use bigger props for Halloween than for Valentine's Day or St. Patrick's Day, so they use very different sizes of boxes.

Being organized will help you as a teacher do a better job. You won't have clutter and it's easier to manage your class if you know exactly what you are going to do each day. You'll be able to grab everything you need quickly and easily, as well.

Instructional Hacks

Need to capture your students' attention? There are a lot of ways to keep their eyes on you, some serious and some silly. Let's take a look:

Wear a crazy hat. You'll instantly catch their attention and they will be watching you the entire class. It's a fun way to get attention and you can make it your thing, wearing a different hat every week.

Use specific praise. Don't just say "good job!" Instead, be specific. Tell them that you're proud of how hard they worked, their perseverance, or their kindness. When you get specific, the students will repeat the behavior because they know exactly what you liked.

Walk around the room. Movement catches eyes and when you walk around, you can be right there next to a student at any moment, so they aren't going to be goofing off.

Add music to the class. Music is a great way to help students focus better. Classical music is excellent for this. You can also play soft music while you do any reading.

Graffiti wall. Give the kids each a dry erase marker and write a topic on the board. They can all go up and write what they know. Alternatively, have one student assigned to the board and they are responsible for writing down what students call out about the topic. This is an excellent way to revisit a topic and review information.

Sit on their desk. If you have someone who is falling asleep or distracting the class, you can walk over and perch on their desk. This is a nice way to let them know you see them and you're keeping an eye on them. It's also very difficult to pass notes or talk when the teacher is literally on your desk.

Use their names. When you're reading a story or telling a math story problem, use the names of your students in the story. They'll immediately start paying attention, because you're talking about them.

Switch up their seating. Have your students sit on top of their desks if they're safe, or move to a whole new seat. It changes their perspective and wakes them up.

Just changing the classroom environment a little can have a big impact on how your students react. I'm always surprised at how much a little thing can change my students' attitudes.

Techniques to Quiet a Noisy Class

Some noise is to be expected in a classroom full of children, but it shouldn't be prohibitive. If you need your students to listen up and pay attention, you will need to quiet them down. This is particularly difficult if you have just completed a fun activity and everyone is hyped up and talking or laughing loudly.

Here are a few techniques that I use to quiet down a rowdy class.

Flick the Lights

You can either turn the lights off completely or just flick them on and off. The visual stimuli will startle the students and catch their attention. If you do this regularly, they'll know that they are expected to pay attention to you now and be quiet. It's also effective because you don't need to be heard over the hubbub.

NOISE Erasure

Write the word "noise" in large letters on the board. Every time the students get too noisy, you erase a letter, beginning at the end of the word. Once they've gotten to the point where it says NO, you will begin to enforce a no talking rule. This gives the students the power to control themselves long before you actually implement the consequence.

If you get to the point where you are erasing the O and the N, you need to let the students know what the final consequence will be. Then be sure to follow through.

Five Finger Silence

If you need the kids to pay attention to you, try teaching them to respect the five finger silence. Raise your hand with all five fingers spread out and wait. You should inform the students the first few times that each finger has a purpose. These are:

1. Focus on me.
2. Be quiet.
3. Stay still.
4. Put whatever is in your hands away.
5. Listen.

In time, they'll see the five finger signal and will quickly calm down to pay attention to you.

Use a Rain Stick

I love my rain stick. It provides a soft, gentle sound that is pleasing to the ears and best of all, it catches students' attention. So, when they're getting too noisy, I simply turn the rain stick over and hold it up. If they can't hear the trickling beads inside, they are being too loud and they know to quiet down.

Of course, you don't have to use a rain stick, anything with a soft noise will work just as well.

Clap Your Hands

A quick and easy method of warning students that they are being too loud and need to return their attention to you is to simply clap your hands. Repeat once and then wait until all eyes are on you.

Call and Respond

This method requires the noise level to be low enough that students can hear you. It's ideal for ensuring everyone's attention is on you, because they have to respond in unison. The first few times, you can write the student response on the board and practice, but after that, they'll remember. A few ideas for calling out:

Teacher: Who dat?
Students: We dat!

Teacher: I've got sunshine
Students: On a cloudy day

Teacher: (school name)
Students: (mascot name)

Teacher: Never
Students: Give up!

Teacher: Ready Set
Students: You bet

Teacher: Hocus pocus
Students: Time to focus!

Teacher: One, two
Students: Eyes on you

Teacher: Piece of pie
Students: Piece of cake

Teacher: Peanut butter
Students: Jelly jam

You can come up with just about any combination you like. Make it specific to your class, subject, city, or school. There's really no limit to how far you can go with this. The students will find it pretty amusing, too.

How to Wow Your Students

Going to school can be pretty boring for your students and even if they enjoy your class and are doing well, it doesn't hurt to surprise them with something awesome from time to time. If you want your students to think you're the best teacher ever, I have a few techniques that you can use to impress them.

Invite a Guest Speaker

Want to surprise your students and make their day a bit brighter? Invite a guest speaker. This doesn't have to be anyone rich and famous, though if you can swing it, that will really impress them. You can invite a parent, another teacher, or a community member to speak to your class. Preferably about a topic you are studying on.

In my classes, I've had business owners come and talk to my students. They show what it's like to use math in the real world. We've also had accountants and bookkeepers come in to explain various types of math uses, like taxes, for example. Just listening to someone besides the usual teacher can make it an exciting experience.

Surprise Them

Once in a while, it's good to surprise your students, in a good way. Have them walk into a classroom full of balloons and tell them you're celebrating their awesome hard work. Take them to a sports event. Go all out and have a popcorn party, or join up with another class to have a game day outside.

These surprises will not only give kids a little break from the usual classwork, but it also helps them form a stronger bond with you. They'll be more interested in talking to you when it's outside of a classroom setting.

Give a Little Gift

Teacher gifts are a common thing these days, but if you give your students a little something for the holidays or when the year comes to an end, you'll really make them happy. It doesn't even have to be anything big. The fact that you thought of them will help them feel special.

Wondering what to give your students? Here are some ideas:

Pencils: Get some novelty pencils for your students that have inspirational sayings on them and hand them out on special occasions.

Stress balls: Help your students stay calm during exams by giving out stress balls for them to hold and squeeze. If you can find one that suits your class topic, get that.

Punch balloons: Students love balloons, so give each on a punch balloon and they can have a lot of fun battling with other students.

Candy: Why not make a paper flower or rocket ship and add a sucker to it? You can even include a tacky saying like "Stay Sweet" or "Suck it up, Buttercup."

Personalized water bottles: These work very well for students and can be made with cheaper dollar store bottles and name stickers or vinyl.

Bookmarks: If you do this, you should look for bookmarks that suit each student's interests or personality. That makes it a bit more special.

Microwave popcorn: Wrap it in a piece of paper that you've decorated to look like Santa, a snowman, or an elf and you have the perfect Christmas gift.

Bubbles: For younger students, you can't go wrong with bubbles and they are readily available in fun little party sizes at the dollar store.

Use your imagination and you don't need to spend a lot of money (it adds up fast when you have multiple classes of students), but can show your appreciation to your students.

School shouldn't be boring. Students spend a large part of their life in school and it should be a place they are eager to go. When you, as a teacher, are able to surprise them and keep them engaged, you have done a good job, making it a happy place for them to learn.

CHAPTER 10

MY FAVORITE CLASSROOM MANAGEMENT TOOLS + LIFE-CHANGING TIME MANAGEMENT TIPS

One of the keys to managing your classroom is managing your time. As a teacher, time management is your best friend. You have so many hours in the day and you really don't want to spend all of them in the classroom or preparing for the classroom. After all, you have other things to do and a life to manage, as well.

It all comes down to setting your priorities and properly managing your time, if you want to be efficient. You may not be able to get it all done, but you can definitely try.

Time Management Tips

Teachers have a lot on their plate. There are a lot of people who think teachers have it easy, but you have to teach all those students, as well as grade papers, plan lessons, and more. This is where time management comes in. However, even with time management, you can't expect to be a superhero. Make sure you give yourself room to breathe too.

Don't focus on what you're not getting done. Instead, focus on what you are managing and stick to what you can get done. Here are a few ways to manage your time a little better and give yourself more freedom.

Create SMART Goals

You need to prioritize what you're doing as a teacher and as a person, so look at your goals. Are they reasonable? Can they be accomplished? You should review all your priorities and decide on the top three. Then create your SMART goals. They need to be:

Specific: What exactly are you trying to accomplish?
Measurable: Can you measure your goal? "100" not "a lot."
Achievable: Is this something you can actually get done?
Realistic: Is it possible to do it in the amount of time you have?
Time-Bound: Give yourself a deadline.

For example, a goal to be a better teacher is pointless, because it has no qualifiers. Instead, you might say you want to play a month's worth of lesson plans in the next week. This tells exactly what you're going to do and by when. It's also a realistic goal if you are working hard.

Make a To-Do List

Don't just write down everything that comes to mind, though, since you're not likely to get it all done. Instead, pick three things that you absolutely must complete. Then add a few things you should get done and finally, list out what you will do if you have extra time.

Make your to-do list the night before or early in the morning so you're ready to go first thing. Then barrel through the three most important tasks on your list and start working on the rest of them. Anything you don't complete today gets moved to tomorrow's list.

It's actually worth setting up a month to-do list, as well, so you can start chipping away at things that are due later on in the month. That way, you don't end up with everything needing to be done on the same day.

Break Tasks Into Manageable Pieces

If you're faced with a huge task, like grading 100 papers, you can end up feeling overwhelmed and stressed. You might find ways to avoid the work and procrastinate until later. This is a big mistake! You'll still have to do the work, but you'll have much less time.

Instead of procrastinating, break the task up into pieces that you can get done in shorter periods of time. For example, you might grade only one class before taking a break. Or you might do 10 papers and then take a break. By making it into smaller jobs, it becomes less stressful and more manageable.

Set a Pomodoro Timer

This is something that can be incredibly useful if you just need to buckle down and work, but keep procrastinating. Set a timer for 25 minutes and just work that entire time. When the timer goes off, set it for 5 minutes and take a break. Stretch your legs, get a glass of water, or play a game on your phone. When it goes off again, go straight into another 25 minute session of working hard. This method of working is great because it forces you to focus entirely on the task at hand for the full 25 minutes. You know you're getting a break, so your mind will actually stay on track.

Say No

One of the best time management hacks I can give you is to simply use the word no. When someone asks you to do something you know you don't have time to do, just tell them you can't. When something is introduced and you are nominated to lead the activity, tell them you aren't able to take on more responsibility right now. There's nothing wrong with saying no and it is necessary if you're going to manage your time effectively. You can't do it all, so tell people no.

Use Your Productive Time

Are you a night owl or an early bird? Everyone has a time of day when they are most productive and you should make good use of that. If you find it easy to wake up early and get a lot done, then do that. If you are more energetic at night, you'll find it easier to grade and work on lesson plans then.

Stick to creative or high energy projects during your most productive times. Other jobs, like organizing papers and sticking things in binders can be done during your lower energy times.

Lesson Plan Efficiently

You can spend hours and hours coming up with a truly amazing lesson plan for your class. However, is it really worth it? When the class will be over in 30 minutes or so and you spent five hours planning, chances are you've overdone it a bit. I try to keep my lessons simple and to the point. Yes, I add in a lot of fun things, but these are activities and ideas that I've collected over the years, bit by bit and have on hand to spice up lessons.

It may help to set a time limit on your planning. You can also download some pretty amazing lesson plans online and use these. It takes a fraction of the time and is often better than what you would have come up with yourself. There's nothing wrong with doing this. It's not cheating, it's just being efficient.

Use an Accountability Partner

If you are like me, you have issues with procrastination. It might seem like a great idea to clean your whole house when you should be planning for Monday, but . . . then Monday rolls around and you have yet to plan anything. Sound familiar? It happens to the best of us. This is why an accountability partner is so helpful.

Your partner can be another teacher or just someone you trust to kick your butt into gear. It usually goes both ways, so you motivate them to do something and they motivate you. Just checking in on each other can be very helpful. If you know someone will be asking how far you got on your lesson plan, you'll be more likely to actually get to work on it.

Each of you should present what you plan to get done in a day or week and then check in periodically to see how it's going. This is surprisingly motivational.

Ask for Help

You can't do everything, so make sure you ask for help when you need it. This may be as simple as reaching out to someone else for an idea on how to get something done, or you might involve parents in preparing for an event, etc. The idea here is not to try and do it all yourself. Get some help and save yourself the mental breakdown.

If you have a teacher's aide, this can be a great way to ensure you get the help you need. There's nothing wrong with asking for volunteers though. I even use my students as volunteers. They can help clean the classroom and keep things organized.

Automate It

There are so many apps and websites that you can use now to help speed up your organization and class management that it would be silly not to use them. We'll be looking at some of these in the next section, but you should always keep an eye out for ways to automate as much as possible. Don't just consider it for school, but at home, as well. The more time you have to yourself, the more well-rounded you'll be.

Reward Yourself

Working nonstop without ever taking a break or doing something for yourself is dangerous. You'll burn out and end up not doing much good for anyone. It's a good idea to reward yourself for a job well done. After all, you'd do it for your students, so why not for yourself?

Your reward can be anything you like. Often, I'll give myself a small reward for finishing part of a project and when I'm done the entire thing, I get a bigger reward.

Rewards might include:

- A food treat
- A night off
- Watching a show on Netflix
- Going for a simple walk
- Getting a new pair of shoes/shirt, etc.
- Going to a sport event
- Taking a regenerative nap

Everyone has their own reward, so look for something that motivates you. Then make sure you actually complete the task in order to earn it.

It takes time to master time management. Don't be too upset if you schedule and plan and then fail miserably the first few times. You need to be realistic and realize that it does take time and patience in order to get the whole concept down and apply it effectively to your life. However, once you start to successfully implement it, you'll find that you can get a lot more done in a day.

Apps and Sites for Classroom Management

Fortunately, in today's world of teaching, we have technology. There are so many apps and websites designed to help you stay organized and manage your classroom that it would be ridiculous not to take advantage of them. There are literally thousands of options out there, so I'm just going to share the top ones that I like. However, if you find something that you prefer, there's no reason not to use it!

Keeping Track of To-Do Lists

There are plenty of options out there that you can use to organize your to-do list. Here are some that I've tried out.

Todoist: Like many lists, todoist lets you prioritize your to-do list, but what I really like is that it helps you stay on top of things with charts and graphs. It gives you a visual way to see what you have done.

Evernote: Another good option for your to do-list is this very useful app that can be shared and added to from any device. It lets you nest tasks, too, which is useful for when you are trying to break them into smaller parts.

Calendars

Honestly, this could be combined with the whole to-do list thing, since they do go hand in hand. However, if you want to lay out a monthly schedule, then these apps are very useful.

Google Calendar: This is one of my favorites. You can color code, combine multiple calendars and sync them to other people's calendars or even share them.

Outlook Calendar: If you're more familiar with Outlook, you might want to stick to that calendar option for your time management. It can be easily shared, as well.

TimeTree: Use this app to stay on top of all your appointments, message friends about your schedule, and manage your activities by day, week, and month.

Teacher Parent Communications

You need to stay in touch with the parents of your students and possibly the other teachers, as well. There's an app for that! Several, actually.

Class DOJO: This lets parents see in real-time how their children are behaving. Teachers can give or take away points for a student and it shows up in the DOJO. Teachers can also send messages to parents directly.

Student Teacher Communications

Need to contact your students or just want to include more technology in your class? These options are a good way to go.

Google Classroom: Google has something for pretty much every occasion. You can create a virtual classroom with this option and assign homework or other assignments on the app. Then grade them right there to keep things simple.

Socrative: This app lets you make a quiz and send it to your students. You can even do this in class and have all your students answer the questions right then and there. It's a fun way to incorporate pop quizzes into your classroom.

Schoology: A bit of to-do list and calendar sneak into this classroom app that students and teachers can access. You'll find it very easy to use and it offers a lot of functionality for a free app.

Lesson Plan Inspiration and Resources

As a teacher, I know how hard it can be sometimes to get inspired. These sites really help me stay on top of my game.

Pinterest: This site is a wonderful, visual collection of all the tips and tricks you could possibly want in your classroom. It basically just collects sites that provide more information, but you can save the info to boards according to your specific interests.

Teachers Pay Teachers: If you're not opposed to paying other teachers for their lesson plans, this site is a great place to find resources for just about anything you can imagine. It's all digital, so you'll need to print things out, but it is an incredible resource, particularly for new teachers.

Flippity: Use this site to make a spreadsheet into flashcards that you can use with your class.

TeacherVision: This app is not free, but it does give you plenty of lesson plans and the ability to download information to use in your class.

Education.com: Need some easy printables? Education.com has a free option where you can download worksheets, or the paid version, which lets you download and print entire workbooks. Everything from coloring pages to math questions is available here.

Don't be afraid to start using some apps in your teaching. After all, as we covered earlier in this chapter, you can't do it all. Having technology help a little can make a huge change in how much you can get done in a day.

CONCLUSION

By now, you should have a very solid idea as to how to manage your classroom. When a class is handled correctly, you will have very few big problems, just small issues that you need to iron out here and there. The information in this book should help you keep it all under control.

Create a Positive Learning Space

The environment in which your students are learning is very important. The props and decorations on the wall aren't necessary, though they may add some whimsy. What really matters is you. Your attitude will determine how students behave in the classroom.

Creating a positive learning environment is essential and as we've learned, this is best done by cultivating relationships with your students. That human connection is often all they need to start behaving better. It's so easy to connect with students just by talking and making yourself human. When you open up, so do they.

For many students, school hasn't always been the easiest place to be and they may have prejudices against teachers or even adults in general. This is very normal, but that doesn't mean you have to be completely separate in the classroom. In fact, you can turn your classroom into a safe place for students to chill out before class and talk to you. Offer them your friendship and respect and you'll see them bloom.

That relationship with your students is so essential. Without it, they won't have much reason to listen to you and if they don't respect you, it can be very difficult to teach. It's even harder to correct bad behavior. Over the years, I've seen teacher after teacher be astounded at how behavioral issues melted away after they made an effort to sustain a real relationship with the students. It's amazing what happens when you talk to them and get to know them. Bit by bit, those walls come down and mutual respect is born.

It doesn't happen overnight, and you'll still have the occasional issue, of course, but it is so much easier to prevent big problems when you can easily get a student's attention and gently correct them. In fact, I've watched many teachers and students grow as they bonded. Once the relationship is established, it's far easier to teach a class full of students. You know each one by name and their interests and hobbies. It makes for a much more rewarding teaching experience, in my mind.

Set Up Routines

Your routines and procedures in the classroom will also contribute to the overall wellbeing of your students. It may be a challenge to teach them all the ways you want them to behave at the beginning of the school year, but you will be very glad you did once they have it all down. Your classroom will work very well on its own and even if you were to leave for a while, your students should be able to continue using the procedures that you have put in place in order to continue their education.

When you share these procedures with your students, you're giving them focus and confidence. They know how things work and they will thrive when faced with the same routine each day. You can add little changes, of course, but overall, students know what to expect and what is expected of them. They will behave accordingly.

You can also use your time management and organizational skills to create a classroom that is more conducive to learning for your students. With the right skills, which can be learned over time, you will find it easier and easier to teach.

You Set the Tone

You are the one who makes your classroom a place to learn. You are the one that the students look to when they need help. If you have the right attitude and build on those relationships we talked about earlier, you're going to have a happy, educational classroom.

Remember, greet those students at the door with a smile and a good morning. Correct them gently throughout the class and never forget to teach them to believe in themselves. These are lessons that will stretch far beyond the time you have with them. If they are confident and sure of themselves, they will go far and even years later, they will still remember the lessons you taught them . . . even if the actual math or English concept is long gone.

We teach for life, not for the moment. Remember that as you

plan your lessons, deal with a difficult student, and stand in front of a loud, boisterous class. You're shaping the minds of tomorrow, so let's get it right.

In this book, you have learned how to relate better to your students, create a lasting bond with them, and how to manage even the more difficult students. This is all something that every teacher should know. It took me a long time to learn it all, but now, I'm passing this information on to you so you can build up a classroom management program that works for you. I hope you have found the information presented here useful and will use it to become a better, more efficient teacher. If you have learned even one technique that you plan to apply in your classroom, my job here is done.

Above all, you need to treat your students like the human beings they are. Focus on the relationship first and the teaching second. You'll cultivate a wonderful bond with these students and you'll see amazing growth over the year. You can make a big difference in your students' lives just by caring about them.

REFERENCES

- 6 Ways Teachers can Spread Intentional Positivity | Rethinking Learning. (2017, October 17). Retrieved September 27, 2019, from https://barbarabray.net/2017/10/17/6-ways-teachers-can-spread-intentional-positivity/

- 7 Classroom Management Apps for Tech Savvy Teachers - Hongkiat. (2019, June 25). Retrieved September 30, 2019, from https://www.hongkiat.com/blog/classroom-management-tools/

- 32 Strategies for Building a Positive Learning Environment. (2015, June 4). Retrieved September 30, 2019, from https://www.slideshare.net/edutopia/32-strategies-for-building-a-positive-learning-environment

- 101 Positive Affirmations for Kids. (2018, October 29). Retrieved September 26, 2019, from https://www.thepathway2success.com/101-positive-affirmations-for-kids/

- Chong, C. S. (2018, February 1). Top ten time-management tips for teachers | ETp. Retrieved September 30, 2019, from https://www.etprofessional.com/top-ten-time-management-tips-for-teachers

- Clark, C. (2019, July 6). 5 Great Classroom Management Tools That Make Teaching Fun. Retrieved October 1, 2019, from https://tech-vise.com/5-great-classroom-management-tools-that-make-teaching-fun/

- Classroom Management: 10 Ways to Deal with Difficult Students. (n.d.). Retrieved September 30, 2019, from https://www.teachhub.com/10-ways-deal-difficult-students

- Connell, G. (2015, June 5). 10 Fun Back-to-School Activities and Icebreakers | Scholastic. Retrieved September 27, 2019, from https://www.scholastic.com/teachers/blog-posts/genia-connell/10-fun-back-school-activities-and-icebreakers/

- Connell, G. (2016, September 15). 10 Ways to Build Relationships With Students This Year | Scholastic. Retrieved September 26, 2019, from https://www.scholastic.com/teachers/blog-posts/genia-connell/10-ways-build-relationships-students-year-1/

- Cox, J. (n.d.). 10 Classroom Management Mistakes to Avoid. Retrieved September 27, 2019, from http://www.teachhub.com/10-classroom-management-mistakes-avoid

- Cox, J. (2019, August 16). 10 Ways to Keep Your Class Interesting. Retrieved September 27, 2019, from https://www.thoughtco.com/ways-to-keep-your-class-interesting-4061719

- Das, A. K. (2019, April 15). Strategies to Build better Teacher–Student Relationships. Retrieved September 30, 2019, from https://theknowledgereview.com/strategies-to-build-better-teacher-student-relationships/

- Elias, M. J. (2015, March 30). Using Humor in the Classroom. Retrieved September 27, 2019, from https://www.edutopia.org/blog/using-humor-in-the-classroom-maurice-elias

- Finley, T. (2014, October 21). 30 Techniques to Quiet a Noisy Class. Retrieved September 30, 2019, from https://www.edutopia.org/blog/30-techniques-quiet-noisy-class-todd-finley

- Gunn, J. (2018, August 29). How to Build a Growth Mindset for Teachers. Retrieved September 26, 2019, from https://education.cu-portland.edu/blog/classroom-resources/growth-mindset-for-teachers/

- Hatch, A. (2018, September 19). 7 Great Strategies for Dealing With Shy Students. Retrieved September 30, 2019, from https://www.boredteachers.com/classroom-management/7-great-strategies-for-dealing-with-shy-students

- Heggart, K. (2015, February 4). Developing a Growth Mindset in Teachers and Staff. Retrieved September 26, 2019, from https://www.edutopia.org/discussion/developing-growth-mindset-teachers-and-staff

121

- Hudson, H. (2019, August 21). 12 Must-Teach Classroom Procedures and Routines. Retrieved September 30, 2019, from https://www.weareteachers.com/classroom-procedures-save-sanity/

- Kelly, M. (2019, January 31). Top Important Classroom Procedures. Retrieved September 30, 2019, from https://www.thoughtco.com/important-classroom-procedures-8409

- Konen, J. (2017, November 14). Managing Classroom Procedures | Teacher.org. Retrieved September 29, 2019, from https://www.teacher.org/daily/managing-classroom-procedures/

- Smith, J. (2017, July 14). 10 Teacher Organization Hacks to Save Your Sanity - WeAreTeachers. Retrieved September 30, 2019, from https://www.weareteachers.com/organization-hacks/

- Stanley, B. (2018, June 21). 7 Tips on How to Make Lessons More Engaging and Fun | Emerging Education Technologies. Retrieved September 30, 2019, from https://www.emergingedtech.com/2018/01/7-tips-on-how-to-make-lessons-more-engaging-and-fun/

- Swartzer, K. (2017, December 6). Using Positive Reinforcement in the Classroom as a New(er) Teacher. Retrieved September 27, 2019, from https://www.learnersedge.com/blog/positive-classroom-atmosphere

- Terada, Y. (2019, February 27). The Key to Effective Classroom Management. Retrieved September 21, 2019, from https://www.edutopia.org/article/key-effective-classroom-management

- Tornio, S. (2019, September 12). 37 Inexpensive Gift Ideas for Students. Retrieved September 30, 2019, from https://www.weareteachers.com/18-holiday-gifts-for-students-that-wont-break-the-bank/

- Watson, A. (2018, April 18). 50 fun call and response ideas to get students' attention. Retrieved September 30, 2019, from https://thecornerstoneforteachers.com/50-fun-call-and-response-ideas-to-get-students-attention/

- Wilson, J. T., & Montoy-Wilson, M. (2016, August 21). Shift Gears to Take a Growth Mindset Approach to Classroom Management. Retrieved September 26, 2019, from http://blog.mindsetworks.com/entry/shift-gears-to-take-a-growth-mindset-approach-to-classroom-management

- Woodard, C. (2019, August 7). 6 Strategies for Building Better Student Relationships. Retrieved September 30, 2019, from https://www.edutopia.org/article/6-strategies-building-better-student-relationships

Made in the USA
Middletown, DE
18 July 2022

69667157R00076